Life's Apologies

Life's Apologies

CAROLANN MURRAY

ARPress

ILLUMINATING IDEAS.
EMPOWERING VOICES

ARPress
45 Dan Road Suite 5
Canton MA 02021

Hotline: 1(888) 821-0229
Fax: 1(508) 545-7580

Ordering Information:
Quantity sales. Special discounts are available on quantity purchases by corporations, associations, and others. For details, contact the publisher at the address above.

Printed in the United States of America.

ISBN-13:   Softcover   979-8-89356-850-9
              eBook   979-8-89356-851-6

Library of Congress Control Number: 2024908983

Table Of Contents

PREFACE

It is not often that we can take note of an instance in which people who have done an unjust to others has in turn apologized to them for their wrongdoings. Being able to own up to their responsibilities by admitting their wrongness and apologizing is why *Life's Apologies* is an excellent choice to read. *Life's Apologies* will encourage people to recognize and perhaps think about possible consequences before committing misdeeds against others. Awareness through *Life's Apologies* will enable readers to face the reality of their consciousness. People who willingly and deliberately commit offenses have a conscience but create a blockage to enable them to do wrong. As a personal choice, *Life's Apologies* can be a truly self-motivating book for anyone who wants to do what is right. It provides transparency to the readers that they are not alone and have a way out that will lead them to vindication and forgiveness. Believing that God has forgiven them will also allow them to experience peace and freedom from bad situations. They conclude that the situation is over and has now became a part of their past. Bad situations will never become a part of the past until people come together and acknowledge their wrongdoings. However, people who choose to read *Life's Apologies* may consider sending others who are offended a copy. This can be done by bookmarking the page that reflects the similarity of the wrongness that they have done. Doing this will assist in bringing closure to wrongdoings and release burdens that they will no longer have to carry. Readers will find that *Life's Apologies* will open doors to forgiveness and lead to a self-fulfilling peace of mind.

ACKNOWLEDGEMENTS

I thank God for enabling me to express myself by putting my creative thoughts on paper. I give thanks to my beloved mother who always encouraged me. Memories of her continue to be a catalyst force in my life.

INTRODUCTION

Life's Apologies is a book about experiences people have endured, either self-inflicted or caused by the hands of someone else. *Life's Apologies* is also a tool that can be used as relief for some who may believe that there is no resolution to their painful experiences, and that forgiving someone and asking for forgiveness are options that could lead to their healing. The purpose of *Life's Apologies* is to be informative by letting the readers know that it is not worth it to go through their entire life committing misdeeds, or holding grudges on the inside, or to never apologize or forgive. Those who do not find peace within their inner-self could cause stress and uninvited fatal medical issues.

Life's Apologies offers support to people by encouraging them to realize that they are not alone, and that apologizing and forgiving are their best options. Although *Life's Apologies* is a fictional book, this book makes numerous efforts to reach out to those who are in need of personal comfort.

Life's Apologies shares many snapshots of similar experiences that may have made some readers feel as though there was no outlet. Therefore, it is important for people to apologize when they done others wrong. Forgive them when they have done you wrong. It is encouraged that prior to mailing copies of this book to intended people, that you bookmark the page that you would like them to pay special attention. It is believed that everyone has a conscience and *Life's Apologies* offers the avenue to obtain forgiveness and inner peace through independent and informal discussions.

Chapter 1

Life's Apologies

When On Door Closes

1 John 1:9

If we confess our sins, he is faithful and just to forgive us our sins, and to cleanse us from all unrighteousness.

Job 36:7

He withdraweth not his eyes from the righteous: but with kings are they on the throne; yea, he doth establish them for ever, and they are exalted.

Proverbs 3:27

Withhold not good from them to whom it is due, when it is in the power of thine hand to do it.

John 7:37–38

In the last day, that great day of the feast, Jesus stood and cried saying, "If any man thirst, let him come unto me, and drink. He that believeth on me, as the scripture hath said, out of his belly shall flow rivers of living water."

New Beginnings

To my grandkids, do not ever think there is not enough time in life to start over and make a new beginning. Sometimes people prevent themselves from starting new beginnings in their lives. They are so tied up with hanging onto the past until they fail to see what is directly in front of them. At the same time, giving up on something should not be confused with starting a new beginning. Remember, some people gave up on moving forward due to previous failures and not being able to let go of the pass. If the failure was forced and uncontrollable, then yes people should have done their best to move forward in their lives.

Those who experienced rape definitely want to move on with their lives. If it was required that they faced their assailant in order to start a new beginning, they would not care to. However, they must forgive and be counseled as they start their new beginning. Another situation could be that a professional sportsman suffered a career-ending injury. In both instances, the rape and the injury, they suffered wounds that would force them to partake in new beginnings. New beginnings to avoid an abusive relationship that is unwanted could also mean the relationship shall be terminated. It is important to have purposely driven new beginnings that would take control of the situation and build self-confidence.

New beginnings to-do list should be developed and completed to assist with staying on track. If they put on their list to start and finish college but failed, this would serve as catalysis for failing all over again. Negative friends or influencers that caused much havoc and had to be removed in the pass as being helpful with new beginnings because they communicated negatively. In most cases, when some have repeatedly failed, they were faced with the prospect of setbacks in self-confidence and the inability to maintain consistency. The ability to start new beginnings meant that people have positively responded to counseling and changed their environment. Being determined to pursue new beginnings is the key to a better life.

All grandkids should apologize and pray for those who believe there is not enough time for new beginnings.So, I am sending you this book in regards to *Life's Apologies.*

Accept Closure

I wanted to bring closure to the traumatic experience that I suffered. I prayed for this memory to end so I could bring closure to that chapter in my life. I feel compelled to share the memory of my traumatic experience because you may have had a similar experience. Each day I struggled to leave the past where it belonged, and I blamed myself and tried to justify the decision I made. This made me want to erase my entire memory, but we know that that is not possible unless it could be proved scientifically that a pill could be produced and taken and as a result, your memory would be wiped away. Unbelievably, many people are haunted by their past and would love to have unwanted memories erased. You cannot erase your memory in order to bring closure to a traumatic event that took place in your life that you would rather not want to deal with.

Wikipedia proclaims, "People who are feeling distressed by unwanted traumatic memories, which they may constantly be 'reliving' through nightmares or flashbacks may withdraw from family or their social circles in order to avoid exposing themselves to reminders of their traumatic memories. Physical aggression, conflicts and moodiness cause dysfunction in relationships with families, spouse, children and significant others."

It could be very complicated to cope with the memory of a traumatic experience. Some people may result to drug and alcohol abuse in order to deal with it. After the first significant incident, my life spun into a downward spiral that continued to descend lower and lower, and it followed me for a long time. It all started at a young age when I thought my friend could be trusted. We had driven and parked in an area so we could be alone and talk. I thought he was a good person and would keep me safe. However, it was no longer than ten minutes before a police officer drove up and asked what were we doing in the area after dark. I stayed in the car, and the person whom I was with spoke with the police officer. I was not in hearing range, but next thing I knew, I was being told that we had to leave the area and my friend left me with the police officer. The police officer said he would escort me out of the restricted area and I was relieved and thought everything would be okay, because I was with the police officer. I sat in the backseat of the police officer's car, and to my amazement, he said that we had to do something before he would take me back. I became afraid and in a state of shock.

All the while keeping his hand on his gun, he then said, "I could write you up for being in a restricted area during the hours of darkness if you do not cooperate." That is when he demanded that I take off my undergarments. He took indecent liberties with me, took advantage of my innocence, and then raped me. The only peace and closure that I found in the memory of this traumatic experience was to accept the fact that I cannot change what happened to me. All I know is that it was crucial for me to forgive those who harmed me, and it is equally important that they be given the opportunity to apologize.So, I am sending you this book in regards to *Life's Apologies*.

A Heavy Yoke

There came a time when people needed to wake up and come to their senses about carrying someone else burden. There were many things that happened that caused people to carry their crosses and sometimes the crosses of others. They worried more about whether they would be able to withstand the tragedy that led to carrying the cross once the tragedy hit home. There was a tragedy that took place when two sons became engaged in an argument and the one shot and killed the other. The reason for the argument became less important, but the basis of it was that the mother was caught in the middle of their dispute. She loved both her sons, but now the one was buried, and she lived on with guilt wondering if her other son thought she felt he should have died instead. Her son asked God for forgiveness, and he told the family how much he regretted what happened. He told them that it was his burden and his alone. Although people were not responsible for the burdens of others, they still took on burdens that did not belong to them. The guilt of killing his brother was a burden and almost unbearable for him. The burden that he had to carry was his and not for the mother. The tragedy of the one brother who killed the other took a great deal of prayer and family counseling to overcome the shock of it. After extended counseling, the mother realized that the burden was not for her. She learned that her mistake was initially accepting that she was responsible for the tragedy. She had accepted the death of one child and continued to love the other and realized that it was not her burden or cross to carry. Right or wrong, no apology would bring her son back. She apologized and asked her family to apologize to each other for the tragedy that they caused and endured. She knew that apologizing would relieve them of a heavy yoke.So, I am sending you this book in regards to *Life's Apologies*.

Opportunity to Move On

Negative feelings of emotions that are felt when you are hurt or offended by another could lead to bitterness, vengeance, and anger. Victimized persons can forgive others by showing compassion because it will help to overcome the adversity that took place. No one is perfect, and mistakes do happen; therefore, it is important to have empathy and the ability to reach out with understanding and have the capacity to show forgiveness. Having compassion could also make way for a new start and a better relationship between those that are involved. People that are allowed the opportunity for growth will learn how to embrace peace and joy after they have shown that they can be compassionate as well as forgiven.

In order for peace and joy to be obtained, you must let go of the resentment and anger because if you do not, it means that you are incapable of forgiveness and your life just became an unhappy nightmare. You must also forgive those who harbored resentment against you, because forgiveness goes both ways, and just because one person has forgiven, does not mean the other should not. Due to an emotional attachment, it is easy for people to harbor resentment and hostility against people you loved or a friend who have violated your trust. Harbored resentment and vengeance could allow negative feelings to take root and fester. You made a conscious decision to refuse to hold grudges and to embrace peace and joy, and it was a great initiative because calmness came back into your life.

When you made your decision, it was good because you are not persuaded by the transparency of others around you, who cared less about having joy. Others will know that you care about the peace and joy in your life because it led to a healthier lifestyle. Your life can be defined when you invite forgiveness, and your health will not be at risk due to negative emotions being held inside. People who can forgive others are able to let go of bitterness and become a better and healthier person. Stay healthy by not wasting your time on harboring anger and bitterness, but concentrating on forgiveness.So, I am sending you this book in regards to *Life's Apologies.*

Chapter 2

Life's Apologies

God First

Ecclesiastes 12:1

Remember now thy Creator in the days of thy youth, while the evil days come not, nor the years draw nigh, when thou shalt say, I have no pleasure in them.

2 Timothy 2:22

Flee also youthful lusts: but follow righteousness, faith, charity, peace, with them that call on the Lord out of pure heart.

1 John 2:15–16

Love not the world, neither the things that are in the world. If any man love the world, the love of the Father is not in him. For all that is in the world, the lust of the flesh, and the lust of the eyes, and the pride of life.

Proverbs 12:1

Whoso loveth instruction loveth knowledge: but he that hateth reproof is brutish.

Prayer Works

I prayed and I prayed that I did not have this incurable disease. But when my test result came back positive, I was so angry that I wooed old girlfriends and new ones. Then I passed on that positive test results to those whom I thought gave it to me. But I continued to pray, hoping that I would get a recall saying that the positive test result had been mistaken. When I learned I had been stricken by an incurable positive test result, my insides became my outsides. I was cheated on by my old girlfriend, who in turn gave me that incurable disease from the other boyfriend. Just as the person who did not care when it was given to me, neither did I care when it reversed back to the cheaters. I felt violated and angry at the world because I knew then that I was stripped of all rights to dignity to be portrayed as a decent moral citizen that society would embrace. I was a good person trying to live a righteous life, but that was taken away from me.

No doubt, a revolver was used to attempt to kill me without having to pull the trigger. I became so resentful at the thought of being killed, that I followed the adage of "Eye for an eye" rather than "Judge ye not and ye shall not be judged." Without doubt, my actions were cruel, devastating and mean-spirited. I took the time to make sure all my victims suffered the same as I had yet, I still prayed for all our well-being. I thank God that we have come a long way regarding medical research for this incurable disease. If not for med-ical research for a cure, my victims and I would be deceased by now.

Nowadays, people who had been stricken with an incurable positive test result can receive medical treatment that may prolong life. A prolonged life may enhance the probability of a longer life because the disease remained dormant for an indefinite period of time. Our only saving grace was we had a chance to live longer than expected. The ill-willed suffering that I intentionally inflicted upon others was too unbearable. Prayer had been my only solution in find-ing peace with this incurable disease. With a world of regrets I beg for forgiveness and I prayed that all my victims will accept my apologies.

So, I am sending you this book in regards to Life's Apologies.

Judge Not

Mom and Dad, I want to say that I am leaving our family church because I am no longer happy being a part of this congregation. I am aware that once I leave our family church, the judging will still linger. Joining another church will give me peace and a fresh start. Members of the new congregation may appreciate and accept me for who I am and the spiritual gift that God bless me with. My gift is the ability to sing and uplift the spirit of those who are receptive toward praising God and embrace my spiritual gift. My feelings do not matter, and there are those who could care less about my gift, yet I love enough to not hurt the feelings of others. I do not always tell everything because I do not want to hurt anyone's feelings. If I cannot share my feelings with my parents, then I cannot talk with anyone. There are other reasons why I must leave this church, so I am not going to hold back talking with my parents. As it stands, people are judging and labeling me as a loose woman who is easy bait for the men, because supposedly I am having sex with a church member who is married and another who is a choir member. It does not matter if the rumors are true, because the accusations alone are damaging and insulting. All I know is people are casting judgment against me for false reasons. I do not know what I could have said or done to put myself in this compromising situation. Some of these churchgoers come to church just to gossip and to accuse me of doing things that are not true. I can barely hold my head high or face the very people who are supposed to be God-fearing. I wish I was judged not for something that is not true. In light of it all, I feel very bad for the embarrassment that I am causing my parents. Please forgive me and accept my apologies for causing embarrassment. So, I am sending you this book in regards to *Life's Apologies.*

Celebrate Joy

Having joy is an individual choice, and you can be happy or sad it is within your control. Being joyful is because of emotional events that you may take pleasure in. There are different forms of emotional events that can create happiness, peace, and joy. Some people receive the Holy Spirit to achieve joy in pursuing God. This is a good start to obtain faith and motivation in the spiritual realm, which often leads to peace of mind. Most people enjoy fellowshipping and making peace with others who are within the congregation. On the other hand, there are others who never find joy. Then there are those who get joy by helping others to celebrate having joy. Helping others is good. Although senior citizens want joy, being able to receive assistance makes life feel like it is worth living another day. Experiencing the death of a love one is emotional but not new. Keeping faith in God regardless of how unfortunate things may be, you should never give up, look to family, and friends for reassurances.

Many families create their own traditions such as yearly vacations, and some gather every Sunday for family dinners, no exception, and in turn create joyful memories. Everyone shows tears of joy when a new member is added to the family. People also find joy when a family member passes on because the person no longer has to suffer pain. More joy comes when that new born has grown up and is graduating from high school. Parents show pride and joy during times like that. Knowing that sometimes kids get in trouble and circumstances stand in the way of having joy. However, trouble and the unlikely circumstances may warrant you going to jail. But through some miraculous act of faith or the grace of God, you were vindicated. All you can feel was nothing but joy, which came after an almost failure. This allows for a joyful life that was based on emotional happiness.

The act of joy can be an emotional event that can be experi-enced and received by anyone who is receptive and is willing to take pleasure in happiness. No matter what the issue or the circumstances, there is always a silver lining of joy in the end. So, I am sending you this book in regards to *Life's Apologies.*

My Life

Practicing celibacy has to do with abstaining from sex, and perhaps marriage, but it is a decision that should be taken seriously. A decision to live a celibate life may not be acceptable by others. It is your choice and right to a solid and meaningful life. Celibacy can be a great sacrifice if you only listen to those who support you. Consult with your pastor for guidance on celibacy, and your sacrifice will be well worth it. While practicing celibacy, it will also be challenging, but being firm will help you to build a solid foundation.

The advantage of choosing a celibate lifestyle is not to have sex, or be involved in an unwanted relationship. Making your own decision will relieve you of undue pressure and obligations. Be certain, negative influences will lead to disadvantages of living a celibate life. For instance, you may have children prior to your decision to practice celibacy, but if you do not, it could be a disadvantage. If married and you both agree on celibacy, then both of you can be happy, even without children.

Nevertheless, when celibacy is based on an existing health issues, it could be detrimental to the marriage. Once this nice couple was going through life-threatening medical issues and was later forced to live a life of celibacy. The wife had a health condition that was diminishing, and the husband had an extremely high-natured sex drive. There was no relief other than to care for his wife whom he loved so much. During this situation, the husband seriously thought about having an affair in order to relieve his sexual appetite. It was too difficult for him to practice celibacy, and at the same time watch his wife faded away. Since he is a person of faith who believes in God, he decided to honor his vows and stand by his wife in sickness and health and until death separates them.

A man and a woman were created and became one flesh and what God has joined together, let no man separate. It was an understanding that the husband was faithful until the end, when his wife eventually passed on. The celibacy for the husband was a disadvantage that was due to uncontrolled circumstances. The advantages and disadvantages of celibacy as a part of having a relationship can be acceptable. Therefore, as previously mentioned, you can build a normal and spiritual relationship for your life, because celibacy is a matter of choice that you make for yourself and not for others to make for you.So, I am sending you this book in regards to *Life's Apologies*.

Lifestyle Rejection

When we say same sex, we automatically assume it is understood as someone being homosexual. I would like to look beyond the stigma of homosexuality and focus on the idea that no one wakes up the next morning and say, or take the role of being a homosexual. I believe that there is always a cause and thereafter an effect. Some will say I was born this way and it is in my genes, and it was passed on to me. If that were the case, I would pose the question, well are the parents homosexuals? Nevertheless, if I prefer the same sex and it did not come by way of genetics, then how did same sex come to be the pref-erence of choice? Some people feel as though there is another person that lives inside, and never found true happiness until the involve-ment with the same sex became an acceptable reality. It is not for me to judge, we are all who we want to be and if not we try. Everyone has a story of how his same sex orientation came about. I would like to share this oddness with you.

One day I asked a young man to tell me his story of how he became the way he is, meaning a homosexual. I never once used the word gay. Well, as I spoke with him and gave him reasons why I would like to put his story on paper, he was quiet and respectful. Therefore, I went on to say that, at one time I felt as though I would never have anything to do with a child of mine who decided that he is going to live a homosexual lifestyle. Then I said how it be that on yesterday, I loved my child, but today since I learned that he decided on the same sex, I hate him. When I shared my view on same sex with him, he gave me a small smile and agreed to an interview. However, the interview never took place and I believe that he is uncomfortable with his attraction to the same sex.

I would also like to point out that if a person chose to turn his back on people because of sexual orientation, it is wrong in the sight of God. God says love everyone regardless and leave the judging to Him. Loving a sibling, relative, or friend who is homosexual does not mean condoning the behavior. That must be between that person and God. Now, how does a person tell his family that he is a homosexual because he is attracted to the same sex? Perhaps I should apologize for not living my life the way my parents feel I should or the way they believe would be a normal life. Please accept me for who I am and continue to allow me to be a part of your heart and life.So, I am sending you this book in regards to *Life's Apologies*.

Chapter 3

Life's ♥ Apologies

I Need You to Survive

Matthew 6:14

For if ye forgive men their trespasses, your heavenly Father will also forgive you:

Matthew 18:21–22

Then came Peter to him, and said, "Lord, how oft shall my brother sin against me, and I forgive him? till seven times?" Jesus saith unto him, "I say not unto thee, Until seven times: but, Until seventy times seven."

Psalms 19:12

Who can understand his errors? Cleanse thou me from secret faults.

2 Chronicles 7:14

If my people, which are called by my name, shall humble themselves, and pray, and seek my face and turn from their wicked ways; then will I hear from heaven, and will forgive their sin, and will heal their land.

Deceitful Friend

I know we were best friends and depended on each other to be there. But I failed our friendship by backstabbing and being deceitful. I was there when our friendship was thought to be great, but most of the time I was embarrassed. I was not a real friend, and since we have not spoken in a while, I realized even more how such a jerk I had been.

Before I can be a positive influence, I must focus on what is meant by being a good friend. Being a real friend means influencing each other to rise higher and become better people. Real friends ensure honesty and are able to be patient and will tentatively listen. There are indicators that will surface, and the other friend will have figured it out whether the friend is being real or not. The friendship should not become a popularity contest; therefore, it is important to know why the friendship exists. A friend out of convenience will become bored then it will be learned that the friend was just an opportunist. Real friendship should be taken seriously and not for granted. Real friends are hard to come by, so trust that real friend will be there at all times when needed.

I did not bring out the best in our friendship, only the worst. A real friend deserves a friend that does not have to worry about being liked regardless of age and background. That friend will also demonstrate good standards and smartness as it relates to an experienced person. In the future, my advice is to stay away from the toxic people who pretend to be a friend when really the friendship was insulting and based on negative talk. Get a real friend who has a good heart, trustworthy, forgiving, and will not show betrayal when mistakes are made.

I learned that Proverbs 18:24 speaks on having a fake friend, because I pretended and did not show myself friendly, and neither did I show that I cared about the things that mattered to us. In all of this I have learned a valuable lesson: I missed our friendship and realized that I was the fake friend with no self-esteem and with an attitude problem. I was deceitful, selfish, and even took our friendship for granted. Please forgive me for my failure as a real friend and I hope my apology is accepted.

So, I am sending you this book in regards to *Life's Apologies.*

No Excuse

She was my rivaled sister, and it lasted through adulthood. With her, it had never been about jealousy. Everyone seemed to have a less than positive opinion of her because she seemed to invite questionable behavior. Even when she entered high school and went on to college, her behavior worsened and became reckless. Talking with her about her behavior seemed to be useless and a waste of time. She was provocative and sexually suggestive. Regardless of how much she acts out, the love between us will always be there. If you let her tell it, she knew what she was doing, and would tell you to stay out of her business and that it was normal for some students while attending college to become one of those girls who offered sexual favors for financial support. It did not matter if the man was much older, as long as she was supported financially. Some people may think that it is okay to date and be a kept woman supplying sexual needs to a man who can pay all their financial debt and also provide a lifestyle of luxury. My sister should listen to what I have to say because she could encounter them again under professional pretense, which she had not been professional. The last thing she should want to be a part of is to have caused a marriage to become broken.

Whether she believes it or not, she is a courtesan, prostitute. Because of prostituting for a married man who is wealthy, my sister is living a life of luxury in a paid for apartment, her tuition is paid in full, and she has no financial debt. There is no excuse for being a kept woman or prostitute, and this type of behavior is unacceptable. There are many students who have worked their way through college and were also funded through student loans. No one wants to be overwhelmed with student loans, but there are some students who also prefer to have respectable and decent and non-challengeable character. It was obvious that graduating from college was important for her, but how she did it was inexcusable. Regardless of the circumstances, forgive me for being so judgmental and critical. Let us move forward as loving sisters, so please accept my apology.So, I am sending you this book in regards to *Life's Apologies.*

Non-Teachable Spirit

The intent of mentoring is to provide coaching and leader management to personnel who are new to the organization. Mentoring can be beneficial to the workforce. The benefit of having a mentor is to ensure mentors, as well as new personnel, are able to develop in such a manner that would provide quality work and job satisfaction. The expectation is to develop skills and support career choices that will ultimately create balance and meet the goals of the organization. If the goals of the organization cannot be met, it is apparent that men-toring can also be a painful and difficult endeavor.

The most difficult aspect of mentoring is to mentor someone who does not have a teachable or learning spirit and therefore are unable to receive mentoring. Likely when people cannot accept mentoring, it is normally due to their "I know everything" attitude, claiming "I have done this before" or "That is wrong, this is the way it should be done." People who are as such tend to carry an air of arro-gance about them. They have an authoritarian-type character and are accustomed to not listening to others and being in charge. This is the same as the new person's character that the organization expects to be mentored. Nevertheless, during mentoring, they usually end in embarrassing themselves, and then in turn have to apologize for their rudeness, thinking that it will immediately make everything okay.

Being a good mentor requires experience, and if mentors do not have the proper experience, they may end up being the one that is receiving the mentoring. Anytime someone steps out of line, initially it is best to accept his or her apology and ask him or her not to allow it to happen again. But when this happens too many times, it is time to let the person go because he has a non-teachable spirit. So I apol-ogize to the person not being able to mentor him.

So, I am sending you this book in regards to *Life's Apologies*.

Not Too Late

I have done nothing but caused pain and sorrow in the eyes of my loved ones. There were times when I stayed out all night and lied when I was late coming from work. When our daughter became ill, I blamed my wife. As my daughter remained on life support, it seemed that there was nothing left that could be done or to hope for other than a miracle from God. I reached back into my childhood and remembered the godly platform that I was raised on, and that my Father had provided through my parents. My father always told me that with God, all things are possible and all I had to do was trust in the Lord with all my heart and lean not unto my own understanding and that He will give me the strength I needed to see me through my pain.

While my daughter lay in a frozen state on life support, I recalled the praying mother that I had. I then fell to my knees at my daugh-ter's bedside, and I prayed to God in the name of Jesus to perform a miracle on my daughter and that I am allowed to go home to glory before my daughter.

I said, "Oh God, I know when You are involved, and I know it is not too late for me to realize the errors of my ways."

I unjustly blamed my wife for our pain, and for that I need to repent and ask for forgiveness for what I allowed to come out of my heart. I asked God to perform a "Lazarus" and bring my daughter back to me. I have always known that God said he would do anything we asked as long as we were obedient. Therefore, I first repented to God for how I treated my wife and then I went to my wife and asked for forgiveness. I told my wife that I had been ungrateful and took our marriage for granted, and that there was no reason that would justify us treating each other as strangers in our home. My wife and I, hand in hand, visited our daughter and learned that God had kept his promised and performed a miracle .My wife accepted my apol-ogy, and our family is unshakeable. We live for God.So, I am sending you this book in regards to *Life's Apologies*.

Sense of Self

To the man that I thought loved me,As long as we were together, I had a sense of self and a positive grip on life because of my love. However, when I thought we were parting ways, I became a nervous wreck and would go out of my way to keep my boyfriend and the love within our relationship. I did anything that encouraged my boyfriend to tell me that I was the only one. It was beneficial for my boyfriend to stay with me because it was the gifts and the money that kept us together. Actually, I should not have used my gifts as a means to not be rejected. I was doing the paying so we could stay together, but sometimes I became depressed, because I could not bear the thought of being left for good. But this one time when I thought I was being left, that was the best thing that could happened because I had been questioning my sense of self and who I was. Then I realized that my identity and sense of self was based on the idea of me need-ing to be validated while sharing my personal space with someone. This taught me that I should have paid more attention to myself and how I felt, rather than being dependent upon someone else. I owed it to myself to make my own decisions and not chase after someone, when I know the person does not want me. I never needed my boy-friend to make decisions for me.

Whether my boyfriend had left me for good or not, I knew it would have been my fault. Because of my low self-esteem, I applied more pressure on my boyfriend than I realized. I thank God, because since then, I learned to recognize my worthiness through my sense of self. I want to apologize to my boyfriend for the pressure I caused, and I thank God for allowing me to gain my sense of self. I hope my apology is accepted.

So, I am sending you this book in regards to *Life's Apologies*.

Chapter 4

Life's Apologies

Emotional Awakening

1 Peter 2:19

For this is thankworthy, if a man for conscience toward God endure grief, suffering wrongfully.

Jeremiah 4:19

My bowels, my bowels! I am pained at my very heart; my heart maketh a noise in me; I cannot hold my peace, because thou hast heard, O my soul, the sound of the trumpet, the alarm of war.

Isaiah 53:4-5

Surely he hath borne our griefs, and carried our sorrows: yet we did esteem him stricken, smitten of God, and afflicted. But he was wounded for our transgressions, he was bruised for our iniquities: the chastisement of our peace was upon him; and with his stripes we are healed.

Hebrews 12:11

Now no chastening for the present seemeth to be joyous, but grievous: nevertheless afterward it yieldeth the peaceable fruit of righteousness unto them which are exercised thereby.

Anger

It is a sad feeling to go through life being angry at the world, angry because you were not happy with yourself or the decisions you have made over the course of your life. Maybe you turned out to be something that you dislike and blamed others for your discontent with your life. Perhaps you are a person who showed no compassion for others; therefore, you also blamed them in order to find relief, and this allowed your emotions to take over and get the best of you through anger. Anger that is pinned inside will result in you to act first and think later, meaning you will act on impulse. Acting on impulse can be very destructive and will cause unnecessary self-inflicted wounds that you will regret later, which could have been avoided. To avoid impulsive anger would be to deal with it by expressing yourself in a civilize manner. You can also release pinned-up anger by forgiving and being apologetic.

It was this person who was remembered for never taking the opportunity to apologize because of being such an angry and hateful person. Being well-known for having anger outburst blew a fused. This person lost control and became a crazed person who made hurtful and destructive comments that could not be taken back. One day this person started yelling and screaming and swearing at this individual for something that the person had nothing to do with. Everyone was on the job working when suddenly this crazed person singled out a coworker during the course of an angry outburst. Everyone in the entire building heard the slamming, the banging, and the belittling and degrading that this crazed person was taking out on the subordinate coworker. It was later learned that this crazed person was enraged because his wife had abandoned him for another man.

By now, you must know that nothing can be achieved through anger and taking it out on innocent bystanders that has nothing to do with the root of your anger. Just so you know there was nothing that could alter the memory of your angry words. But if there is a chance that you may read this, you should know that there is no ill feeling that is held against you. No matter where you are, I forgive you and accept your apology.

So, I am sending you this book in regards to *Life's Apologies*.

Trapped Inside

My brother, I am so ashamed of who I think I am and what I turned out to be. I violated my precious niece and traumatized her. I molested her and dared her to say anything. It was not the first time I had molested someone. After molesting my niece, I became scared and I moved to the other side of town. For years, it has haunted me because I knew what I did was wrong, wrong, and wrong, and I know you would not have done it to my daughter, your niece. I am a disturbed person, and as a result, my conscience is eating me like a cancerous tumor that affects my mind and my nerves. I do not know what to do. I feel so trapped inside of a cage. My mind is filled with pressure and the thought that one day you will be told of what I did. My emotions have been tied in bundles for years, and my pain is as a bottomless pit that will not stop trapping me.

I love you and know that it does not dismiss the egregious act that I had committed. I needed someone who can help me understand my problem and how to untangle my bundle of emotions. I am so tired of feeling as though I am trapped inside of a dark tunnel. If it had happened to my daughter, I would probably hunt down and beat the person in the ground until I could no longer swing or kick.

My brother once this is read, I expect to get what I deserve. I am overwhelmed with regret. My sorrow and regret was that I did not open up to my brother about my horrible impulsive actions, and neither did I share the thoughts of being trapped in my mind before the molestation took place. Acting out my sexual act did not relieve me of feeling trapped inside of my mind. I just want my brother to know that the other reason why I am apologizing is because it is a part of my healing process. I am hospitalized and I want to get well and take responsibility for what I have done. Please forgive me and accept my apology.So, I am sending you this book in regards to *Life's Apologies*

Age Gracefully

To the younger and prettier friend, you need to know that life as you • age is time spent on earth, but when you say age, it is about people aging and being able to adapt. There are times after aging, when the next thing you know, you are physically and emotionally old. Aging is a natural process that cannot be avoided, but there are some people who will try. It is obvious that some people do not accept the aging process because emotionally, the minds become deprived. It is an emotional and a self-conscious habit to check every strand on your head, diet when you do not need to be dieting. Makeup is plastered on too thick, and yet you are still not satisfied with your almost perfect and beautiful appearance. You have an emotional complex regarding your aging appearance.

Regardless of your profession, and looking like a super star, you will age and there is no denying it, so be smart and embrace aging gracefully. How you feel about age determines whether you will walk into old age with grace or not. No matter how old you become, it does not mean you are not beautiful just because you are not pictured the way others think you should be. It does not give anyone the right to disrespect you because of not accepting your appearance. People should appreciate the uniqueness that they possess and be thankful.

To be candid, there are people who would rather look older and be respected according to their character than worry about physical appearance. It is not about what a person look like as much as it is about the attitude, dislikes, or being displeased with what they see in the mirror. Normally, those who appear as snobs that toss the nose in the air then look down on others are unhappy on the inside. In order for you to shield your unhappiness and the ugly personality that you possess, you feel the need to deceive your aging process by getting a Botox procedure. Botox will make it seem as though your aging is a normal slow process. Remember, aging is a reality, and Botox is external, whereas blueberries are internal works from the inside out that will slow down the aging process. Eating blueberries will also make you feel better about yourself and your age.

Aging is a process, and some people fail to respect it for what it is, and therefore cause embarrassment in order to save their physical appearance by relying on other means in attempt to slow down the process. The sooner you learn about physical appearance and not judge others because they have grown old and have aged, the sooner you can save yourself the embarrassment. Accepting life as you age is better. It is only natural, and nature cannot be avoided. God has blessed people to age gracefully; therefore, to the younger and prettier friend, you need to apologize for not embracing and disrespecting the aging process.So, I am sending you this book in regards to *Life's Apologies.*

Man Up

My mom and girlfriend refused to realize that I am a man. The problem that my mom and girlfriend had with me was I resisted being dominated. My girlfriend never had a problem with me smoking the entire time we lived with my mom until now. There are women who would rather have a man that sat at home all day and do nothing without any purpose in life. It has been hard for me to live under the same roof with both women who wanted me to bow down. I am a strong man that has been pulled in two different directions. Every time I turned around, one or the other felt it was okay to tear me down. When I refused to be pulled down or persuaded during intense arguments, I was told to get out and leave. It seemed I have outlived my welcome and it was time for me move on. I am ashamed, because these women never understood the value of a good man. If women knew how to woman up, some problems would not exist.

I am not unmanly by far and I learned long ago how to be a man and to man up. If I were submissive and behaved as anything other than a man, I would never be allowed to man up. When the men tried to be men, women would expect the man to crawl under a rock or in a corner. When I worked and paid the bills, it was never enough. My girlfriend consistently degraded me and tear me down in front of my son. The next day, as sure as the sun rose, I left. I had o leave because there was no way I could have stayed another day. My mom and girlfriend did not want me to leave but I left anyway. I knew if I were to be a man and do what was required of me, I had to man up. Therefore, I had to leave, so please accept my apologies for leaving.So, I am sending you this book in regards to *Life's Apologies*.

Trapped in a Box

Everyone at some time or another needed to cry and or cried. The ones that did not cry were trapped inside a box. Because of misfortune, they failed to communicate and open up about their pain. So much pain pinned inside and tears caused by a relative who continued a generational curse. No matter how twisted, it was hard to accept that someone could abuse a child. The child was threatened and made to sit in a corner and when the mother came home. The molester would tell the mother that the child did not do her homework. Secretly, he looked at her in a crossed way, daring her to tell. The child cried as she sat on the floor in the little square corner. She was always overwhelmed by sadness, fearful and withdrawn, and slow to speak. Her mother screamed at her and asked her why she did not do her homework. She was still trapped in a box and even her teachers inquired about her being withdrawn and not sociable with the other students. When she got home from school and the relative was there, the same thing would happen again. She hated home and regretted ever being born, and she resented her mother for not protecting her.

As she became older, she was more isolated and depressed, because he continued to molest her at any chance he could. Then one day, the mother came home early and caught him molesting her daughter. If a child says she was molested, the parent should believe her. This was finally the daughter's way out of being trapped. Her mother took her to the doctor, and there were signs of stress to the private parts of her anatomy. When asked, she said he forced her to touch him. She was given an outlet from a terrible situation and was able to move forward in her young life and found the key that released her from being trapped. Had her mother not came home unexpectedly and caught him in the act, she may not have believed her daughter if she told her.

Children are not able to articulate things unless they have been exposed to them. In this instance, the child is no longer trapped and can move forward with her life. The relative was convicted for his crime, and both he and the child were released from being trapped in a box. He cried and tried to apologize to the mother and daughter.

So, I am sending you this book in regards to *Life's Apologies.*

Chapter 5

Life's Apologies

Work Smarter

Proverbs 17:17

A friend loveth at all times, and a brother is born for adversity.

Proverbs 18:24

A man that hath friends must shew himself friendly: and there is a friend that sticketh closer than a brother.

Ecclesiastes 4:9–10

Two are better than one; because they have a good reward for their labour. For if they fall, the one will lift up his fellow: but woe to him that is alone when he falleth; for he hath not another to help him up.

Proverbs 27:17

Iron sharpeneth iron; so a man sharpeneth the countenance of his friend.

Self-Sufficient

Employment is something that most people want, especially when they have the obligation to take care of their families. It is obvious that people who lack employment have an uncomfortable and less inviting life. They are extremely restless and encounter problems when they do not know if they are be able to care for their families. When people rely on government support, it is still not enough. Their children do not have adequate food at home, and the only other means of eating is while attending school where they receive free breakfast and lunch. Parents also experience a culture shock when they encounter problems associated with transitioning from having a job to not having a job. Parents must then adapt and face the reality of being on the verge of foreclosure on their homes and becoming homeless. They no longer have the friends they once had, and their extended family can only provide limited support. If people can survive through unemployment, this can prevent the separation of families and a downward sparrow of devastation. This devastation reflects the differences between unemployment and employment, and both can be a drastic life-changing situation that places people in social classes. The social classes then become that of a lower class or an upper class.

Searching for and obtaining employment can be as a needle in a haystack and described as being at the bottom of society's unemployment list. It is a part of the lower class. If people are qualified and still cannot get a job, the only thing they can do is continue to search for employment. Once the job search is over, employees can keep their families together and reap the benefit of receiving medical care while being employed. Employees can also provide for the needs of their families and prevent further hardships from being unemployed. The employee can receive additional training that could lead to promotions and therefore can become self-sufficient. Employed people are also self-sufficient and may become a productive part of society. Being a productive part of society makes them vital and they are more likely to achieve the American dream of having a home and not being homeless.

Numerous people search for employment so they may have a better life. Employment can make all the difference in having a better lifestyle.So, I am sending you this book in regards to *Life's Apologies*.

Hidden Agenda

You should love the job that you are doing, and it will be less stressful and easier to excel. Being less stressful will help you to stay focused on what you intend to achieve while working for the company. While working for any company, it is important to be proactive and to maintain excellent job performance when it comes to trying to reach your promotional goals. Ensure you have valid documentations so that you can remain certified and within your job position. As long as you remain certified and demonstrate positive work ethics, it will increase your chances promotion. Continue to be a productive performer and take notice of your strengths and weaknesses. Additional training in your not-so-strong area will help you to create balance within your performance. Do complete all job requirements. And no matter what, avoid gossip and the strategies that people may apply in order to gain an advantage over you. On-the-job friends may have hidden agendas, therefore it is important for you to not be misled or entertained by unhappy and disgruntle employees who has nothing to lose. They only want to make you lose your job because they are disgruntle and jealous employees who have nothing to gain by helping you. Standards and ability to effectively communicate with your manager will create your office mates' opposition and havoc just to stop your inevitable job promotion. However, until you get your pro-motion, continue to maintain your good reputation as a professional worker who is dependable and always deliver on time. When you deliver on your job performance and help the company to achieve its goals, you are also ensuring your job security. Establish a good relationship with your manager and stay the course with regards to your productivity. The quality of your work will speak for itself, and your record will tell whether you deserve the job promotion regardless of the opinions of others. Your employers will see through the plot of those who do not wish to see you get the promotion. Regardless of the opposition, employees must meet the requirements if they want to receive a job promotion to the next level. The other employees who plotted against you are the same ones who will apologize to you once you receive your job promotion and become their manager.So, I am sending you this book in regards to *Life's Apologies*.

Cooperative Teamwork

Teamwork can be looked upon as a group of individuals or employees that have come together and form a team in support of a business. It takes a great deal of effort to be a part of any team. A team consists of two or more people, and I believe that the more people that are on a team, the more difficult it is to hold the team together. My reference to team does not necessarily mean a sports team; it could be a team that is a part of an organization or an office environment.

First and foremost no matter how small the number is that makes up the team or how great the number is the point is it takes much effort on everyone's part to keep it together. Therefore, it takes a great deal of compromise and willing attitudes that comes together for the good of the team. In every team there must be a leader, someone who has the attributes and knows how to manage others. The team will only be as effective as its leader. The team's leader will ensure that each member is trained and knows what and when to do what is needed to be done. As the team functions together, they must also show respect and be sympathetic toward the special needs of the others. Without consideration toward the team members and the responsibilities, the organization will lack complete control and will eventually crumble. The team personnel must interact with one another and demonstrate high performance and exercise much disciplinary.

Teamwork can be one of the most positive experiences if everyone works together. It is the unique personality that each person possesses that may be the root of causing conflict in various areas of the team.

For example, if teamwork is a major factor while embarking upon a business venture, it will take the cooperation of everyone involved in order for it to be successful. The worst thing could happen is to have a selfish member of the team who does not care about working together to enhance a smooth operation. Unfortunately, this will lead to infighting, disagreements, and a disaster. Overall, teamwork can be a positive element to a business proposition. It is always better teamwork when a team of two or more can work together in harmony.

So, I am sending you this book in regards to *Life's Apologies*.

Homeless Family

Sometimes an opportunity is not recognized until it is too late. When opportunities arrived under favorable circumstances, the right decisions must be made in order to embrace the existing opportunity. People have at times mistaken opportunities as just being luck. However, people are given opportunities in various ways and forms, in that to be given an opportunity because of volunteering to serve your country. The chance to conduct an interview of a high-profile person whom most journalists wanted but were not given is a serious opportunity. There are also people who were called opportunist, because of doing anything to get an unfair advantage at the expense of others. Once the advantage is achieved, the opportunist created an opportunity by stepping on others to get there. Nevertheless, a husband received an opportunity for a job promotion that required relocation of the family. The job promotion opportunity was turned down, and the family decided not to relocate. Six months later, the husband got caught up in the company downsizing and was laid off. It did not take long for the family car to become repossessed and the house to be foreclosed. The family became homeless and had to live with the husband's family. The husband failed to accept the job promotion opportunity that also included all-moving expenses paid in full. When a company downsize in one location, it is likely that it created job opportunities in another. The husband regretted the predicament that the family was in and went on to apologize to everyone for being homeless.So, I am sending you this book in regards to *Life's Apologies*.

Courage and Bravery

It takes a strong heart, determination and a willing attitude to succeed what you want in life. Because of the lack of understanding of who you are, there are times when you may turn out to be your worst enemy. You must be able to control you own destiny, meaning that you must have the ability to set the goals that you would like to achieve. No one can put a wedge between you and your goals, or hopes or dreams if you do not have any. Once you have taken control of your destiny and have a plan to accomplish your dream, it means that you have learned how to demonstrate self-confidence and possess the courage and bravery it takes to follow through.

Along the way to achieving your dreams and goals, you will find that there are some people who will hate on you. As long as you believe in yourself, that all things are possible with God, you will be able to maintain your determination. The last thing you should do is fight against yourself and buy into the negative influencers who do not want to see you make it. You are the deciding factor in your life and should be persistent and always go after what you want. When the odds are against you, your strength and toughness will help you to fight back and not allow anyone to steal your dreams.

If you want to be a doctor, a lawyer, or an astronaut, some will tell you, "Oh it is going to be difficult, and you are going to be in school and training forever." Your response should be that of firmness. Showing that you have tenacity by saying, "I do not care what it takes this is my dream and I am going to do what I have to do to succeed." At the same time, you are also saying that you will not compromise what you believe in and you will absolutely stand by your convictions. Sometimes when others are just as persistent as you by continuing to drive wedges between you and your goals, they are only being negative toward your desires. They will continue to be negative influencers or make all the excuses in the world as to why you should not pursue your dreams. Remember to never give up on your dreams for the benefit of others, just to make them feel good or to be a part of a clique. Stay tough, do your own thing, because your determination will define your purpose and reasoning.

Most people do not understand that they themselves can be their worst enemy when it comes to reaching any goal they chose, but if they maintain power and determination over themselves, they will succeed. As long as you show that you have fortitude and guts, you will never fear or forget the power you have over your own determination.So, I am sending you this book in regards to *Life's Apologies.*

Chapter 6

Life's Apologies

Socially Speaking

Deuteronomy 8:18

But thou shalt remember the Lord thy God: for it is he that giveth thee power to get wealth, that he may establish his covenant which he sware unto thy fathers, as it is this day.

Deuteronomy 28:1

And it shall come to pass, if thou shalt hearken diligently unto the voice of the Lord thy God, to observe and to do all his commandments which I command thee this day, that the Lord thy God will set thee on high above all nations of the earth:

Deuteronomy 28:13

And the Lord shall make thee the head, and not the tail; and thou shalt be above only, and thou shalt not be beneath; if that thou hearken unto the commandments of the Lord thy God, which I command thee this day, to observe and to do them:

Isaiah 40:31

But they that wait upon the Lord shall renew their strength; they shall mount up with wings as eagles; they shall run, and not be weary; and they shall walk, and not faint.

Psalms 121:1–2

I will lift up mine eyes unto the hills, from whence cometh my help. My help cometh from the Lord, which made heaven and earth.

Social Judgment

Social skills start at a young age and are then developed into experiences, interactions, and the obvious behavioral reactions that it is made. Some people thrive to interact with others so they can prove themselves sociably. However, others grew up in a less fortunate environment, go off to college, and would now work for a firm. They will distant themselves from the past social skills that was introduced during their childhood through learning and seeking social approval from others on their adulthood. They want to fit in with the people that they must socialize with. However, they must exercise interpersonal skills in order to effectively operate in the confines of the organization.

People who have natural operating people-person skills do not take much effort to effectively communicate. Having interpersonal skills, being able to listen to others at the right time, the ability to persuade others as natural leaders will tilt the scale in positive directions. Those who do not have interpersonal skills will tap into their emotional behavior and social skills. Since their skills are learned, it is still possible for people to reach their goals through training and reinforcement of their behavioral skills.

Persuasive behavior will also play a role in influencing others to enhance their interpersonal skills. People who are not Blue-collar workers but are in leadership positions also have interpersonal skills and social approval from the people in their work environment. They strengthen their behavior through enforcement, which will enhance the choices that are made based on social skills or behavior. This could also mean the difference between positive and negative influences, which may also turn out to be judgmental. Social judgment weighs heavily on attitude and behavior. Therefore, people may be judged by the effective listener's attitude. The effective listener wants to change the attitude of others, hoping that positive persuasive influence will be enough to change their negative behavioral attitude. If the attitude cannot be changed, social judgment then carries consequences. People then tend to make comparison by using their personal views and ideas on what type of attitudes are acceptable.

There are people of past traditions that neglect their social information because of authoritarian mindsets and chosen truths that impact their social skills and behavior. People's ego will have an effect on their lives and attitudes. Ultimately, the two concepts are people's attitudes that are based on their past and present experiences, and that affect their social judgment. People's social skills are derived from their childhood experiences that are coupled and developed with current behavioral concerns. Social judgment is delicate because it may be influenced by social skills that take on major roles in overall life experiences. .So, I am sending you this book in regards to *Life's Apologies.*

Dissimilarities and Inequalities

There are those who would say that there is no injustice and all is well, but others would say the opposite. Injustice can come in many forms, and separate entities do not want to be singled out as being unjust. If there was no injustice, the world would be closer to being perfect. Injustice acts depend on how a situation is responded. The law enforcers may use excessive force, and when the force leads to brutality and unlawful death, a suspect status is then changed to victim. This is when the authority and actions of the law enforcers becomes questionable. The less fortunate ones are forced to band together and question the legitimacy of the law enforcers.

The color of a person's skin should not be a factor (but maybe it is), nor should the ones who have the power and authority be allowed to have influence over law enforcers after a decision has been made. Some will have you believe that if you have wealth and is not of color, you may get by with a slap on the wrist rather than being brutalized by excessive force or murdered. If the policies are legally enforced, it will minimize the amount of undue scrutiny that may be received by the law enforcement officials. Police will then be able to do their jobs while doing the right thing, and those who break the law should be punished. Law enforcers will be able to do the job with minimal interference from the public.

Same as law enforcement, the economy can demonstrate in society on how injustice can be in favor of those with wealth and less forgiving toward those who are poor, to include government officials. People who are poor tend to have a less than favorable opinion of the government. Largely because the government will not allow an increase in minimum wages and continuously changes the rules on what percentage should be paid, and yet the wealthy continues to get wealthier. The wealthy complaint about food stamps for the poor, but they do not make mention of the yacht that is floating on the ocean floor, and its owner receives tax-free deduction.

The ones who have the money has the power. They have the power to allow the poor to die slowly from the lack of medical care. The responsibility to medical care lies with the government and the people. No one wants to single out a specific person or group to be labeled as injustice; however, it is a proven fact that we do not live in a perfect society. The poor is receiving unjust treatment on all fronts because the government, the ones that hold the power and authority and large bank corporations, they lacks funds. The justice system is tying the hands of the poor and giving the wealthy and the power players' free reign. Save the apology and fix the problem.So, I am sending you this book in regards to *Life's Apologies.*

Blame the Government

When we think government, we reference the people who have ran it, or the way a community was governed. Working people kept the government running because a portion of the income earned was contributed to the funding for government assistance programs for unemployed recipients. However, people that rely on government assistance may not be employed. We cannot blame people for receiving government assistance because of being physically or medically disabled. Thorough and effective screening should be done on those who stayed at home for an extended period collecting government assistance. Devalued environment and social conditions are reasons why the government is needed to do better. Those who are employed are required to financially support the local, state, or federal government in the form of fees or taxes.

Yet, cycle after cycle, the government provided a financial BandAid for the overall economy instead of fixing the problem. It was apparent that there are a limited number of jobs to go around, because if there were more jobs, it would fix the problem. However, there may not be any jobs available for those who are unemployed because of being over or under qualified. Some, on the other hand, had no intentions of getting a job and continued to live on the backs of others. Living on the backs of others also meant that these same people will receive funds from the Social Security Funding Program. For the most part, if people pay into Social Security, then it is right to be paid back. The government should have taken control and cleaned up the economic problems that we are faced with. The government should apologize to the unemployed for failing to create more job opportunities and to the employed for not increasing the minimum wage.So, I am sending you this book in regards to *Life's Apologies*.

Privileged Environment

I looked down on and degraded persons who wore lousy clothes that were badly worn and who had to work part-time while attending this prestigious university. I knew by the appearance and the parttime job as assistant to the university's librarian that this person had to be financially strained. While enrolled at this university, I had no respect for these people. I was taught to stay away from those who barely made it financially. If a person is poor and unable to be financially secured and independent, that person should not be allowed to attend any university such as this one. Although it was not always about the finances; it was more so about being intelligent and smart. I since learned that there are those who received a full scholarship due to a higher level of intelligence.

My level of intelligence was not what got me into this univer-sity. I am not academically intelligent like the less fortunate person who was accepted to the university on a full scholarship. I envied this poor person for having something that I did not have academic intelligence. My parents paid my way and that was how I was able to enroll in the university. No matter how much it cost, my parents paid for everything, to include the best tutor. I had no desire to do better because I was not taught the value of home training, as well as how to treat those who were from a less fortunate environment; therefore, I treated this person like a loser. I was not familiar with life in an environment that would not have allowed me to wear the best clothes, live in the best house, and have the best professor. In fact, I never knew life outside of my privileged environment could be so disappointing. In my environment, I was accustomed to everything being handed to me. This person had to work hard for everything, and that alone encouraged me to develop respect for the differences in both environments. I apologized for my lack of respect and horrible attitude toward this person for not being from a privileged environment. I would like to befriend this person and ask that my apologies be accepted.

So, I am sending you this book in regards to *Life's Apologies.*

Slave Mentality

It is possible that some people do not know what slavery is or what it means to have been enslaved. A person and a culture can be enslaved. The laws and the acts of past slavery laid the foundation and set the stage for slavery to transcend into a modern society with self-inflicted wounds that never healed. Those who were enslaved by the past society passed their experiences of slavery down their generational line. Their physical and emotional abuse became a part of their culture. This enslaved abuse became a way of life for them. During their time as slaves, they were invisible to those who were unlike, and by law superior to them. They were there physically, but not seen. They were only recognized through demands and instructions, and thereafter they remained invisible. They were treated a certain way and molded them into who they became. Their traditions continued to be pasted on to their off springs, and as their traditions were past down, boundaries were crossed because inequality laws were broken and laws for equality were established. It was then that the slave mentality and the effect it had on the individual became transparent.

As society changed and became more modernized, so did its effects on the individuals. Jim Crow of the past became a modern Jim Crow for some individuals of a particular culture. Although inequality changed to equality and liberty and justice for all, Jim Crow became more sophisticated by way of his strategies and euphemisms. The leaks of the past Jim Crow was nothing more than a society that upheld two separated laws one for the enslavement people and the other set of laws for everyone else. Jim Crow's societal self-inflicted wound was as a result of unfair treatment of enslaved people. The impact of the wound was great because Jim Crow left his brand on the backs of those that were a part of his captivity. The trials of the old Jim Crow could be recognized in the modern Jim Crow, because the offspring carried with them the residue of their enslaved parents. The modern Jim Crow was even more shielded and protected because the unequal treatment was disguised, and therefore became invisible to the naked eye. The unwritten rules for the modern Jim Crow also led to disadvantages to society as a whole.

Slavery is not just a time of the past; it is also modernized and is coupled with enslaved climate and goals to continue the disadvantages for the less fortunate ones. Unfortunately, the modern society is suffering from the residue of slavery and must pay into programs that will not enforce equality, and disband laws that support a climate of keeping less fortunate ones bound through slave mentalities. This will enable those who have a slave mentality to be place on the same level playing field.

So, I am sending you this book in regards to *Life's Apologies.*

Chapter 7

Life's Apologies

Healing Heart

Jeremiah 31:34

    And they shall teach no more every man his neighbour, and every man his brother, saying, Know the Lord: for they shall all know me, from the least of them unto the greatest of them, saith the Lord: for I will forgive their iniquity, and I will remember their sin no more.

Philippians 3:13–14

    Brethren, I count not myself to have apprehended: but this one thing I do, forgetting those things which are behind, and reaching forth unto those things which are before, I press toward the mark for the prize of the high calling of God in Christ Jesus.

1 John 1:9

    If we confess our sins, he is faithful and just to forgive us our sins, and to cleanse us from all unrighteousness.

Revelation 21:4

    And God shall wipe away all tears from their eyes; and there shall be no more death, neither sorrow, nor crying, neither shall there be any more pain: for the former things are passed away.

Spare Me Please

I am very upset because of taking care of this woman who is my mom. Somebody spare me please from my mom. I am so tired of transporting my mom back and forth from one place to another to include doctor's appointments. Anyone can call me ungrateful because of all that my mom has done for me, and the fact that I want someone to spare me. I do not know who my dad is, I have no siblings, I am a college graduate, and all I want to do is live my life. Now I must put my life on hold just to take care of my mom. Never once did I think that I would not be able to move on with my life because of having to take care of my mom. My mom and other parents should think to prepare for the end of life inevitable. Instead, my mom solely depends on me for everything, including daily needs, because the reason for my existence is to provide a safety net. Since my mom distanced and divorced us from our extended family, we are left alone.

It is apparent to me that when my mom passes on, I may be left alone with no other family and merely the same circumstances as my mom. So there is no need for me to feel sorry for myself because I am used to being alone, and now that I am more conscious of it, I need to focus on doing what is right. My mom would not have ill feelings toward taking care of me, so neither should I when it comes to taking care of this woman. My life is my mom, and it is my responsibility to be there and do all I can to honor my mom so our life may be easier. I ask God to spare me please by forgiving me for not wanting to take care of my mom. I am sure my mom could sense what I was feeling. Therefore, I am apologizing and praying that my mom will forgive me. Mom, spare me please and accept my apologies.

So, I am sending you this book in regards to *Life's Apologies.*

A Father's Repentance

The father of his children tried to do the best that he could to ensure that they lived a decent life. Most people know that things do not always go as planned. For him, it meant no job and no medication, and this caused the father to revert to previous problematic disorder or behavior he experienced in the past. There was this one time when the father was unable to purchase his medications, he became suicidal and had to be placed in an institution until he was able to deal with his emotional setback. He had an emotional relapse disorder that was contributed by and associated with a traumatic memory of fragmented sensations. Before he was placed in the institution, he unsuccessfully tried to kill himself and his children.

The father regretted what had happened because his son had to be hospitalized and the other two children lived with his sister. The father expressed being torn over what he had done, and the fact that he does not remember everything that transpired. He knew his children were embarrassed to call him dad, and they did not want to be in his presence. His wife died in a hit-and-run car accident. Therefore, he wanted to do whatever it took to make things right between him and his children because he is the only parent they had. This father was aware that the children were afraid he would have another relapse, but he assured them that his treatment had ended and he has recovered. The father also wanted them to know that he is medically well and have a job.

So many times the father prayed to God when he needed to find a job so he could make things better for his family. He needed his children to know that he could be trusted, and he will do anything to put the family together again. So he prayed to God for healing and repentance, and forgiveness. This father also prayed that his children will accept his apologies.So, I am sending you this book in regards to *Life's Apologies*.

Losing A Parent

When a parent is diagnosed with cancer, it is a difficult and heart-breaking experience that no one would want to endure. When a parent is suffering from cancer, it weighs heavily on the children and the people around that person. Regardless of what stage of cancer or whether the person is in remission, it is still in the memory of the children that they could prematurely lose their parent. It is better to be in remission than stage four to have to deal with the constant pain, which may be managed by medications, radiation treatment, or chemotherapy. It is difficult for children to watch their parent endure severe pain. The pain is no joke, and the children become very emotional and realize they must adjust their everyday schedule in order to meet the needs of their parent. Children must be committed to their parent, because their action will have a lasting emotional effect on them. Children should also be present during the entire ordeal and be ready to make decisions that will relieve the suffering as the end of life approaches. There are many responsibilities, and not everyone is equipped to handle. Deciding to keep the parent or not is one, and if so, who will be there. If the parent cannot stay at home, do you use the nursing home or a hospice center as options? Children become overwhelmed with responsibilities for making arrangements. Lives will be rearranged because of work schedules, but someone has to step up and be the caretaker.

Having to face these responsibilities and watch the life escape from the parent will cause children to lash out at each other. Siblings have their own way of dealing with grief. The family must reach out for spiritual counseling and remember that God will heal and deliver their parent from the pain. When your parent has passed on and after they are delivered, that is when you truly learn that being born of the same womb does not make you family. After passing on but before the parent can be buried, siblings become defensive and will turn on each other. Family will grieve and argue at the same time over who can have what property or money instead of coming together. Truth be told, there will always be one who will take the lead on planning the funeral, and being the family peacekeeper. This sibling will also encourage the others to share memories to keep their emotions under control because everyone is grieving even if it does not appear that way.

Family become emotionally overwhelmed as they go through the grieving process during the suffering of their loved one and after the loved one has died and passed on. Family also realized that cancer being the cause of their parent's death will have a lasting effect on them because it is possible that their life could end as a result of the same cause.So, I am sending you this book in regards to *Life's Apologies*.

Embrace Grace

Since it was within my control whether I received this illness, I decided not to do what was right. I was careless, and as a result, I acquired my illness because I willfully came in contact with it knowing it could have been avoided. I chose to do what I wanted and became ill because I allowed my partner to transmit to me an incurable disease. I did not care about the pain and suffering I caused because when my family tried to tell me about my partner. I ignored the fact that my partner was not as forthcoming about being positive as I was led to believe. I followed my emotions, and that was when my life was derailed onto the wrong track.This was the same as with Adam and Eve. Eve did not make Adam take a bite from the apple, and neither did my partner make me. Doing what someone else enticed me to do was my choice. I did this to myself. I failed myself and now I have tested positive for an illness that can be controlled but not cured. I cannot blame anyone for me doing what I was told not to do. My mistake had two owners, and both were at fault, but it was a cold-blooded person that knowingly exposed me to a com-municable disease that caused my illness. I broke the hearts of people who loved me, and not one time did I consider the importance of what they told me because I put the value of my partner first. I cannot say that the love that I received was worth the sacrifice because I will pay a grave price for something that could have been avoided. I made a choice that I will have to live with.

Putting the virtues of my partner before my own left the impression that I forgot what it meant to have faith in God, and to do His will. I also failed to show wisdom, courage, and hope. My family said that I was smarter and always showed the courage to stand up for myself and knew what it meant to have principles. I worried about if I would be judged based on my principles, or would saving grace through God allow me to be redeemed. Having my illness proved that I tested positive and did not take my virtues seriously; I failed to show the courage to stand on my own principles.

Take it from someone who has experienced it. There is no way anyone could go through what I have and withstand the pain. My family told me to remain strong and accept the consequences of my actions. If only I had embraced grace and listened to those who loved me, I would have seen a sign of relief. I ask for forgiveness and I apologize for the affect my illness caused others. So, I am sending you this book in regards to *Life's Apologies*.

Chapter 8

Life's Apologies

I Am a Woman

Genesis 29:32

And Leah conceived, and bare a son, and she called his name Reuben: for she said, Surely the Lord hath looked upon my affliction; now therefore my husband will love me.

Exodus 20:6

And shewing mercy unto thousands of them that love me, and keep my commandments.

Deuteronomy 7:12

Wherefore it shall come to pass, if ye hearken to these judgments, and keep, and do them, that the LORD thy God shall keep unto thee the covenant and the mercy which he sware unto thy fathers:

Luke 7: 48–50

And he said unto her, Thy sins are forgiven.

And they that sat at meat with him began to say within themselves, Who is this that forgiveth sins also? And he said to the woman, Thy faith hath saved thee; go in peace.

Unlawful Practices

I hate to admit this, but because of poor judgment, I have to live a lifetime of regret. I was pregnant when my boyfriend and I decided to have an abortion. We were still in high school and had hopes of one day attending college; we were not prepared to be parents at such a young age. We wanted to keep the abortion a secret, so instead of going to my mother for help and advice, my boyfriend and I decided to get an abortion at this clinic that was located out of town. Several years later, I learned that the abortion clinic that I used was not certified and closed down due to unlawful practices. The abortion procedure performed on me was botched and now I may never be able to get pregnant or carry a child to full term. Since then, I learned that there were several health centers that performed abortions that I could have gone to. They would have ensured I received the best medical attention possible. Most health centers required patients receive counseling by a certified counselor, and they ensured that patients knew the process and the risks that are associated with having an abortion. For instances, had I been counseled, I would have been made aware of possible complications such as hemorrhaging or the danger to subsequent pregnancies. As a result, I attended counseling because my abortion had an adverse psychological effect on me. Finally, I told my mother of the abortion. I went on to say, "It was the evening before, and during the time when I was too sick to go to school, that I had the abortion." I apologized to my mom for me not coming forward, because there was a time when nothing too sensitive that we would not discuss. Mom, please forgive me and accept my apology.So, I am sending you this book in regards to *Life's Apologies.*

Prostitution Tribulation

Prostitution can be a dangerous profession that some people will run to in order to escape abusive relationships they may be involved in with their family. I heard of a person who escaped from an abusive relationship she had with her father. He would beat her repeatedly, rape her, and then confine her to the house. Her mother was not supportive and provided no help because she was always drunk. When her mother was sober, she cursed her out. She always knew when her father would attack her. Her stomach became tied in knots, and she started to shake uncontrollably and then she would find a dark corner of her room and sit on the floor. Her mother came in the room and stared at her and then she slapped her crossed the face and left. Next her father entered the room and all she could do was scream as she was being raped. This time, she thought, would be the last time.

Very early the following morning, she escaped the house unnoticed. She saw a girl she recognized that had just gotten out of a car and was standing on the corner. They greeted and that was how she got into the world of prostitution. She had her reasons for escaping and felt that anywhere was better than where she had come from. A year had passed and she felt better about herself. She was relieved that there were no more beatings or raping, and that her mother was not around to curse or blame her for what her father had done. Every time she turned a trick, she felt wanted and received a lot of attention from nice lonely men. She did not have to worry about being beaten, and they paid to have sex with her.

She was embraced by her pimp. He would make love to her, give her money, and made sure she had nice clothes and never went hungry, as she had when she was home. Being a prostitute saved her life, but inside she knew selling her body was temporary and she wanted more out of life. She also thanked God for her issues and decided that it was time for her to move on. She thanked God her pimp kept her safe. For the first time, she went to church and gave her life to the Lord. She became saved because she believed Jesus Christ died on the cross and forgave her for her sin.

Finally, she escaped from an abusive family and she put prostitution in her past so she could move forward with a positive life. Sometimes things happened for a reason to get people where God wants them to be. Prostitution can be an unexpected, dangerous profession that some people run to in order to escape abusive relation ships. She had escaped her home and found comfort in the most unusual place that led her into the arms of the Lord.So, I am sending you this book in regards to *Life's Apologies.*

Obedient and Humbled

I do not know how many times I have to tell my mom that I have things to do, places I need to go, and I just want to live my own life. I truly do not believe that I was born for the sole purpose in life to grow up and take care of my mom just because I am able. I know there are times when my mom needs my help, but I do not care. I want my mom to please just find someone else to help because I refuse to be burden down with things that has nothing to do with me. Maybe if I had a brother or sister, we would not be having this conversation or this problem. I am so tired that every time we have this conversation and disagree, the first thing I hear is, "Son, please be obedient and humble, otherwise the number of days lived will be lessened, and God said that." Then I would say, "Mom God did not say to treat a son like a slave who is not on payroll." I am young and I like to have my fun day or night, but I hardly have friends because I have to take care of my mom. Laugh out loud and give me a break.

Well, my mom gave me a break, and said, "Here take this money and go out and have some fun because I can remember when I was young, I liked to have fun too. But the difference between us, son, is I never once disrespected my parents. Son, take this money and go have some fun. I will be alright."

I do try to do more for myself. I can talk, walk, and take care of my personal needs. However, I am guilty of no longer being able to drive or not having friends to fill an empty void. My son is now in the hospital and is suffering from a back injury due to a stray bullet that grazed the spine and he is now paralyzed from the waist down. As I visit my son, while entering the hospital room walking with my four-legged walker, I see a tear-streaked face with apologetic guilt written all over it. My son realizes that a person does not have to be old and cripple to become obedient and humbled. My son is now recovering and is walking again. One thing for sure, I do not have to ask for anything, because God has forgiven my son and provided a second chance to become obedient and humble. Of course, my son asked me for forgiveness and apologizes for the way I was treated. I accept our apologies every day of our life."

So, I am sending you this book in regards to *Life's Apologies.*

My Ovary

Menopause is a matter of fact that comes along with the aging of a woman. There is no way to avoid it. The irregularity of the menstrual cycle may be the first warning sign of early menopause. Menopause is not a disease; menopause is a group of symptoms that are prevalent in women and is jump started by the decrease in estrogen level. Related symptoms can extend to hot flashes, which causes the body to overheat. Other symptoms are mood swings, night sweats, decrease in sexual interest, lost of hair, and memory loss, among others that are not mentioned. These symptoms are experienced by women during the mid and latter part of their lives. Menopause can sometimes start earlier than normal and can last for at least two years. It is possible that some women would have preferred to be born a male rather than endure to all the changes that their bodies must undergo while maturing into a young and thereafter middle-aged woman.

Human nature has charged women with being able to have a menstrual cycle for the purpose of childbearing. It seems that when the childbearing cycle has ended, then the onset of menopause begins. What makes menopause such an unwanted health necessity that women prefer to live without? While referring to the aforementioned symptoms, women can only feel miserable and uncomfortable during the menopause cycle. The question is what can be done about menopause is there a preventive measure? In order to cope with menopause and get through the process, women may be pre scribed meds that balances the hormones during this middle-age phase in their lives.

There is no way to prevent menopause, because it is a way of life for women. However, treatment for menopause varies according to women's needs. As a resolution, sometimes women succumb to hysterectomies as a measure to minimize their discomfort. There are supplements that can also be used to help relieve the discomfort of menopause. Although the symptoms may be relieved, menopause is something that women will have to live through. It is better for aging women to remain conscious for the onset of menopause and accept it as a way of life.

So, I am sending you this book in regards to *Life's Apologies.*

My Sparkle

People may go through life and never realize that they were born with a sparkle. At any case, the sparkle is something they were born with was recognized by their parents while the child was at a young age. The sparkle is not something that is asked for; it is there during birth and lives on the inside. For example, the great Tina Turner was born with a sparkle. As a young girl, she sang in the choir and no matter how hard she tried to tone down her voice, it still dominated the other voices.

A sparkle is something that also stands out from among others. Nevertheless, everyone has their own sparkle. It may not be a musical niche, but the sparkle shines through the eyes and will light up. Every sparkle is different, and people may be unaware that they have a sparkle, and therefore failed to understand what made them different from others. Now the time has come to accept the sparkle, but it is what is done with it that will make the difference as to whether the sparkle will shine. Once the sparkle is identified, it is very important to embrace it as an extension of self and to prepare for what is to come. The sparkle must be fined-tuned by continuous training and grooming. As the person grows older the sparkle becomes more refined, and with much work, the person stands out among the best.

Everyone is responsible for their own sparkle, and if it is taken care of there will be no need to worry, it will shine. Remember, those who do not want to accept the sparkle, they are known as your negative critics. What is important about this sparkle is that it is a gift that belongs to the people. The reward is the vessel that was chosen to be used to carry the sparkle. Do not be afraid of the sparkle. There are those who saw it long before it was developed. As it is nurtured, it will reach its full growth and potential when least expected. The reality of the sparkle is that most people welcomed it because of its shine. Never allow people to talk negative about the sparkle. It must always be protected and handled with grace, especially when it shines. Some people may never grasp that all through their lives, they carried a sparkle that was not allowed to shine. The sparkle is closed to the vessel that it traveled through, and no one would know better than the sparkle. So, I am sending you this book in regards to *Life's Apologies.*

Chapter 9

Life's Apologies

Family Tree

Matthew 6:14

For if ye forgive men their trespasses, your heavenly Father will also forgive you:

Matthew 18:21–22

Then came Peter to him, and said, "Lord, how oft shall my brother sin against me, and I forgive him? till seven times?" Jesus saith unto him, "I say not unto thee, Until seven times: but, Until seventy times seven."

2 Chronicles 7:14

If my people, which are called by my name, shall humble themselves, and pray, and seek my face and turn from their wicked ways; then will I hear from heaven, and will forgive their sin, and will heal their land.

Psalms 19:12

Who can understand his errors? cleanse thou me from secret faults.

Grounded and Rooted

No one can say that being a parent is easy. However, it can be rejoic-ing if you are up for the task and the success you will receive in the end. Your success will depend on the success of your child. Parenting will start from the day the child is brought home from the hospital until the day of total independence and marriage. Before the child comes home from the hospital, a parent should look for resources that will ensure the health and safety of the child. Specifically, with prevention of Sudden Infant Death Syndrome, parents must have an approved crib and remove anything that could contribute to child suffocation such as blankets or toys. Further protect your child by using childproof cabinets and the appropriate safety locks and latches. You may also consider a childproof gate for stairs if appropriate for your dwelling area. As your child grows older, ensure the child is also surrounded by the right people who are being screened and will take part in your child's life. No numbers of concerns are too many when it comes to the safety of your child. As your child continues to grow, it is important that you instill home training and values during your child's upbringing. These values will become embedded and will be a part of development that frames the child's character. Parenting also includes ensuring that your child receives the best possible education. You as a parent must show interest in your child's education and social activities. Keep in mind that what a child learns at home will be taken into the world. Based on how well the parent train and teaches the child and involve him in social activities, will allow the child to excel in life. Your child is then ready to depart the safety of the parents nest. Your parenting should include making sure that your child grows up to be responsible and that you were a positive influence. Parents should always prepare the child for long-term life experiences and as a result, the child will be ready to embrace life. After all you have done as a parent, your child can always refer to you as a reference book.So, I am sending you this book in regards to *Life's Apologies*.

Ungrateful Sacrifices

I was a good person and believed in helping family by making sacrifices. I sacrificed myself by putting many things that I wished to accomplish on hold so that my family could live a better life. While I was making sacrifices, I forgot who I was and what I wanted to be in life. I recognized that I had lost apart of myself because I failed to make sacrifices for myself before sacrificing for others. My sacrifices were considered to be a self-inflicted weakness, and my family started to take advantage of me. The problem with my sacrificing is, when I gave all that I could with nothing left to give, I became a dumping ground. After I made many sacrifices, I was treated as though I was the one who was indebted and obligated. On the other hand, I was given butts to kiss, rather than being appreciated for sacrificing a pair of redbottomed shoes in order to pay for a semester of college. Nonetheless, my sacrifices seemed worthless because I had to deal with selfish family members who always looked to me with out-stretched hands for the next dollar. The advice I gave family members was unaccepted, because of reluctance to accept individual sacrifices or responsibilities. It was as though no one cared and the sacrifices I made were in vain and became a distant memory.

Do not expect to be thanked for sacrifices that were made so family goals could be achieved. Now that the goals have been achieved, the majority did not care, because my sacrifice was an entitlement. For the ungratefulness and selfish spirit, I am very angry, because while I was sacrificing, the clock continued to keep time and never stopped .It was never a waste of time for me to sacrifice for the needs of my family. I do expect an apology for being ungrateful for the sacrifices that I made.So, I am sending you this book in regards to *Life's Apologies*.

Embarrassed Family

This family is the most important entity in the son's life. His parents worked hard and made numerous sacrifices so they could continue to succeed in life. The parents worked two jobs and were able to send their son to the best schools. Their son was a rising star, two years ahead of his grade level and interning while in high school. The parents were prominent public figures within the city and earned their duly respectable appointments. Their son embarrassed them because he committed a gruesome act that overtook their family. To this day, their son regretted what he did.

It was during that summer when both families decided to go on vacation together. All was well until they left the daughter and son to themselves while the parents attended a play. While the parents were gone, something came over the son and took away his sound mind. That was when he lost his mind and ripped and tore the clothes from the daughter's body. He raped and brutalized their friend's elementary-aged daughter and only child. Her screams did not stop as he continued pounding and brutalizing her. Regardless of the son's brutality, with exhausted effort, she continued to fight back. Without remorse, the son left the daughter on the couch.

The following morning police officers interrupted the son and his parents. They were questioned by the police, and the son admitted to doing something but could not recall the event. The parents allowed the police officers to transport their son to the hospital and then he was later committed to an institution for the criminal act that he committed. Being committed meant nothing compared to the physical and emotional affect the daughter had endured.

Due to the daughter's injury, she suffered tremendously, and her treatment and therapy lasted many years. No matter how much he did to try to make it up to his parents, he could still see how embarrassed and disappointed they were. The sacrifices his parents made so that he could have the best were not worth it. He apologized to the other family and hoped that someday they would forgive him. The son also apologized to his family for his crime and the embarrass ment he caused and promised never to commit such an act again.So, I am sending you this book in regards to *Life's Apologies.*

Our Legacy

The act of forgiveness may be a tall order for some people depending on what has to be forgiven. When a son has to ask two mothers for forgiveness, as well as forgive himself, he can be overwhelmed. The impact will be whether they can forgive him. A mother has lost her son at the murderous hands of another and now he wants forgiveness for his act. The mother of the murdered son is overwhelmed with grief, and surely her forgiveness will not be easy or occur right away. At the same time he is asking his mom to forgive him because he must suffer the consequences of the horrendous crime that he committed. His mom will never see him alive on the other side of his incarceration. If only he had listened to his mom and her advice and guidance, he would not have to die in prison.

He understands that he must do life sentence without any chance of parole. His deliberate crime of murder cannot be undone, and his punishment fits the crime. Now it is a choice that he must live with, but receiving forgiveness from the other mother and his mom will make it easier for him to live out his conviction. His incarceration alone will change his entire lifestyle, and he is the only one to be blamed that he will not see the light of day. He is an only child and does not have a child of his own. His mom hoped was for him to have a son so they could carry on the name of his deceased father. With having a life sentence to life in prison, it is unlikely and impossible that he will be able to carry on the family name.

It is unbearable, knowing that his mom has lost her husband, and now her son because he will spend the rest of his life in prison. He still pleads for mercy and forgiveness from both mothers for the pain that he has caused. There is no explanation good enough when someone is murdered; it is inexcusable. Neither is there any amount of apologies that will raise the dead or is acceptable at this time. He wants the other mother to forgive him and his mom to stand by him because it will make his life sentence easier knowing that he at least have his mom. Only the mothers who lose a son at the hands of a murderer or by incarceration without a chance of parole know their grief and feel their pain. He just wants to apologize and hear his mom say she forgives him for the pain he caused.So, I am sending you this book in regards to *Life's Apologies.*

Be Honorable

The intentions I had were less than honorable, and it ruined our business relationship. To put it bluntly, after I was hired to be an administrator in the cooperation, I took the advantage of our respect and trustworthiness. We were both highly respectable persons, and everyone liked us. I was never the respectable and straightforward person like everyone thought I was. We had been best friends prior to the cooperation being launched, and that is when I was bought on as someone that could be trusted. I betrayed our trust and walked all over your unstained principles. All the while, greed was on my mind and dollar signs in my eyes, and that is when I developed a scheme and started taking money from the customers by overpricing equipment and pocketing the profits from my illegal price increase. No one was aware because every cent the business earned was accounted for and the illegal price increase was hidden. It all boiled down to me profiting twice because I was also on payroll and there was no paper trail on the hidden illegal price increase that I received. I created a false payroll and gave it a ghost name that appeared to be credible.

A few years later, the cooperation was audited and no one could explain the pricing or the additional profit gained, or even how it was attached to the funding of the cooperation. Later, after an inter-nal investigation ordered, it was learned that other businesses were being gouged by the cooperation under false pretense and a nonexistent extensions of the cooperation. Therefore, one of the executives was forced to resign because of false evidence and being responsible for faulty business practices of the cooperation. I want my friend to know that I framed the executive, and this made me a less than honorable person. Because I was not honorable, the cooperation faced financial penalties, debt, and burdens. I am returning all the money that I illegally obtained back to the cooperation. I have also resigned because it was the right thing for me to do. I have proved to be a less than honorable person as a friend and employee. Please forgive me and accept my apologies.So, I am sending you this book in regards to *Life's Apologies.*

Just a Contract

When we say marriage, we automatically assume that two people have agreed to bond their relationship and made it a contractual agreement through the court system. The two became married and are emotionally attached; however, the honeymoon fever has subsided and is long gone. As much as we hate to admit, marriage can sometimes be looked upon as a fantasy and a forever after Cinderella tale. Let us get real. Marriage can be hell, and a marriage with kids can be worst, especially when the kids have suffered because no one seemed to care.

I recalled this one couple appeared to have the best marriage, and then one day infidelity penetrated the family. First it started with the husband, then the wife was angered by it all and wanted revenge. Eventually the children became an afterthought. The physical and emotional abuse set in, and neither husband nor wife wanted to live under the same roof or accept responsibility. This marriage was no longer picture-perfect, and something had to be done. The wife realized that the kids were being battered and decided to be the bigger person. She tried to repair the broken pieces. Counseling was inevitable if the marriage was to be salvaged. The problem in this marriage was both the husband and the wife allowed others to enter their sacred marital circle. The family was virtually broken apart and now must be mended back.

No one should ever think a marriage is perfect. That would be like saying life is perfect. What led this couple to believe happiness could be found outside the marriage was taking each other for granted and not giving the attention that was needed. Maybe it was just pure temptation and lust. Although affairs may be common, this does not mean an affair should be included as a part of any marriage. The intent may be to never have an affair, but when more time is spent with a coworker, the attraction will fester. It could have been with the best friend of a spouse or someone that was met online. Either way, it is a painful situation on all that are involved. If an emotional need has not been met, a spouse sooner or later will result to whatever to fulfill the void. One or the other spouse will be unfaithful and betrayed by the other. At this point, both spouses must decide if the marriage can be restored. It will take more than trust, forgiveness, and apologies to ensure that the emotional needs of each spouse are met. Each spouse is responsible for the happiness and survival of the family.So, I am sending you this book in regards to *Life's Apologies*.

Chapter 10

Resist the Devil

Ephesians 4:32

And be ye kind one to another, tenderhearted, forgiving one another, even as God for Christ's sake hath forgiven you.

Colossians 3:13

Forbearing one another and forgiving one another, if any man have a quarrel against any: even as Christ forgave you, so also do ye.

1 Kings 8:50

And forgive thy people that have sinned against thee, and all their transgressions wherein they have transgressed against thee, and give them compassion before them who carried them captive, that they may have compassion on them:

Psalm 79:9

Help us, O God of our salvation, for the glory of thy name: and deliver us, and purge away our sins, for thy name's sake.

Unconscious Deed

I had no reason to live with myself, and neither did I have purpose. Due to my cravings for alcohol, I had lost control over it. It controlled me. When I was drunk, I thought everything was normal, but my normal to others was my drunkenness. I did a lot of things and blamed it on being drunk, but on the other hand, I protected my drunkenness and tried to defend myself. So I could feel good and be satisfied. I reached the point to where I stayed drunk and was reckless. I did not care because there was no reason for me to do better than what I was doing. I was defiant and adamant about my purpose in my life to wake up morning after morning to get my alcohol. My drinking and drunkenness was my only recourse, and it served as a means for my escape for every day of my life.

My reckless behavior was not an eye-opener for me; it was just the beginning and led to self-destruction. I did not seek approval or acceptance because it was not about acceptance; it was more about me recognizing that I gave myself no reason or purpose in life to live for. It was not until one day I recalled myself hitting something I thought to be a deer while I was driving my vehicle. I blacked out and fell unconscious and still I did not care. All I knew was that I caused pain to something and was not going to worry about it. However, in the back of my mind, I felt bad about the accident. When my brother told me that our neighbor was in the hospital because she was hit by a vehicle and the driver fled the scene, I started to think. When I saw her, I suffered more for her pain and also my own pain, and she also suffered for the lifetime pain that I inflicted upon her. My drunkenness became worst and would not go away because someone else is paying for it, and the lifetime pain belonged to me because I invited it.

This Sunday morning, I woke and decided that I am tired of being a drunk and want to surrender. Just like the Bible says, confess your faults one to another and pray that ye may be healed. I confessed and told her that I was responsible for her being crippled that I felt guilty and I apologized to her and asked for her forgiveness. She told me she forgave me a long time ago, and that she was glad that I came to my senses and no longer have to accept destroying a life or living with a heavy heart or guilt. I am the person that did not want my life to evolve, but through the grace of God, I was able to see the light from the sun and the light that made me want to live with myself. Apologizing and asking for forgiveness for the tragedy I caused has put me at peace. I have apologized and made amends so now I can finally live with myself.So, I am sending you this book in regards to *Life's Apologies.*

Stressed and Confused

Please take heed that if it does not matter who you are and where you are going, it does matter how you are going to get there. It is important to be aware that hell is on earth, and if you chose to have a better life, my advice to you would be not to harbor any ill will against anyone and to live and let go. To let go is to repent your sinful shortcomings, and the wrong that you have done others. People will go through life harboring hatred, animosity and will also be vengeful toward another. It does not pay to treat others wrong all your life and then when you become ill and on your sickbed, you decide that you want to start apologizing and asking for forgiveness. Yet, you have a few days while you are on your sickbed to think of all the dirt and wrongdoings you have done to others.

You may remember the time when you were engaged in an affair with your friend's wife, and your friend chose not to see what was going on because of his love for his wife and family. He does not want to end the marriage only to let another man raise his son. So, did you really think the husband did not know you were sleeping with his wife? Your conscience has dug a hole for yourself that you may not be able to dig your way out. Now you are lying on your sickbed and want to set your conscience free by releasing the truth because you realize that hell will have a negative impact on your life if you do not repent. You could have had a happy life with your own wife and family, but instead, you choose to intrude in another man's family. Well, at your request, the other man is at your bedside so that you may ask for forgiveness and be set free. Although you are unable to speak as before, there is no need for you to waste your precious breath on another woman's husband. The husband now encourages you to repent of your transgressions against God, him, and his family. This man forgives you and wants you to recover, repent and live your life in peace. The husband accepts your apology and wants God to forgive you so you may live.So, I am sending you this book in regards to *Life's Apologies.*

Child Protection

Parents be careful of who you allow to be involved with your children. As parents, it is your responsibility and obligation to ensure the safety and welfare of your children. If you leave others to play the parent role in your children's lives, they will do it. When you learn that your children may have been abused, it will be too late to cry about what you should have done. Now is the time to develop an open relationship and candid discussion with your children. Your children must be taught not only to stay away and not speak with strangers, but to also be conscious of possibilities that may land them in abusive relationships.

To prevent children from a closed mindset, parents should explain to them the types of abuse you are referring to and what is meant by child molestation. Teach your children to protect themselves not to be so willing to accept gifts, money, or a free ride home. You will not be around your children every second of the day; therefore, they need to know how to protect themselves in your absence. It is believed that if children understand why, then they are more likely to follow your instructions, especially if they know you will listen to them. They will learn not to be so trusting and that you will always come to their aid. Children will also be ready to protect themselves from strangers and would-be child offenders and you will not have to worry as much. However, it is not always the stranger on the streets. It could be that friends you entrusted your children with, the least expected one, are the molesters. They could be the babysitter, the team transporter, or the coach. Do not allow people to take the power away from you by entrusting your children with them. Do not be fooled by long-time friends of the family or relatives. When abusers are caught, you must take the word of your children. They only know what they learned and are exposed to by the abuser. Trust what your children tell you, because most molesters are savvy enough to talk themselves out of it.

So take your blinders off and support your children. Children are vulnerable and they may be afraid to tell what happened, so you must still report the abuser even if it is a family member, a long-time friend, or stranger. Ensure that your children receive the necessary counseling. It does not cost anything to be protective of your children, and if you do not play a role in their lives, someone else will. Do what is right when it comes to your child. Your children will remember if you did nothing to stop the abuser. Forgiveness and apologies may come after time-served for the personal abuse on children.So, I am sending you this book in regards to *Life's Apologies*.

Rebellious Destruction

Mom, I can remember the time when I brought tears to your eyes and disbelief to Dad's face. I was unstable, very miserable, and found myself being disastrous. I insulted my friends and the boyfriends too. I learned that I was miserable because no one ever paid attention to me, and my parents had always pressured me. My parents nagged me to do this and that, now I am enraged. I lashed out and did not care if I hurt anyone's feelings. I never got any satisfaction hurting anyone's feelings, but it was my way of lashing out when I felt threatened. I became fed up with my parents constantly telling me that I was a good daughter and I would make something of myself. Then the next thing I heard was I needed to work on not being so vocal because it could be damaging and destructive.

Some people failed to realize that the words comes out of their mouths also comes from the heart. Some tend to accept what came out of the mouth as truth, and then failed to realize the defiled words are what caused the turmoil. The last rebellious destruction I created between my parents caused turmoil, and I faced the error my destruction. After the turmoil, it was evident that our family was more important than the rebellious destruction that almost ripped apart the fabric of our family. I wanted to attend an all-night party with my friends, but my parents refused and took away my car keys. When my parents decided not to let me attend the party, I became irate.

Without thinking, I said to my dad, "If mom can go on an all-night party with her boyfriend while you are on business trips, I should be allowed as well." Immediately I realized that my tongue became a double-edged sword and took the life out of my parent's marriage. My dad became the responsible person. To this day, neither my parents nor I spoke a word of my accusation toward my mother. I love both my parents, and I am sorry for my rebellious destruction. Therefore, I am apologizing, and I hope my apology will be accepted. So, I am sending you this book in regards to *Life's Apologies.*

Freedom Over Betrayal

To attempt suicide is a strong indication that the person is in search of help and does not know how to find a way out of being trapped. There are various reasons why a person would attempt suicide. A person who finds that the only way out is suicide is possibly looking for an emotional outlet, in search of relief from betrayal and pain. This caused helplessness, strong feelings of anger or rage, and perhaps a sense of being unloved.

Some people find it more difficult to deal with the issue such as divorce, most especially if they learned the affair of their partner was with someone of the same sex. This apparently was a major blow because the suicide attempt was the answer, and it indicated a feeling of emotional pain and disparity that was endured after learning the truth. This betrayal that led to divorce also meant the spouse possibly fell out of love. It is obvious that the suicidal person blamed himself because his spouse left him for someone of the same sex. It was a matter of coming to terms with a spouse who was homophobic and caused a great deal of hurt.

The best thing that should take place at this point is to obtain a professional therapist who can provide assistance for this person to make a change in his lifestyle. In order for them to make progress and move on, they will have to decide whether he wants to live or not. Through the process, they will learn that there are plenty other reasons to live for other than one person's betrayal.

When a person decides to attempt suicide, one of the indicators is not only depression, but the person will be malnourished as in not properly eating or taking vitamins. During this time of need, when a suicide attempt has taken place, it is important that he realize that he can achieve freedom by living and that he does not have to experience death.

A critical element to having professional counseling is to also have the full support of family. Family involvement is very crucial within the first six months of the suicide attempt. Hopefully through professional counseling, the person can make peace with himself by achieving freedom, accepting the betrayal for what it was, and identifying multiple reasons to live. Therefore, a person may attempt to commit suicide for reasons such as to find relief from betrayal, pain, or a sense of being unloved in order to achieve internal freedom. Nothing is worth someone taking his own life. Prayer and suicide hotline is another way a person can chose to ask for help. So, I am sending you this book in regards to *Life's Apologies.*

Chapter 11

Life's Hurdles

Matthew 10:39

He that findeth his life shall lose it: and he that loseth his life for my sake shall find it.

Proverbs 10:17

He is in the way of life that keepeth instruction: but he that refuseth reproof erreth.

1 Corinthians 2:4–5

And my speech and my preaching was not with enticing words of man's wisdom, but in demonstration of the Spirit and of power: That your faith should not stand in the wisdom of men, but in the power of God.

Proverbs 2:1–6

My son, if thou wilt receive my words, and hide my commandments with thee; So that thou incline thine ear unto wisdom, and apply thine heart to understanding; Yea, if though criest after knowledge, and liftest up thy voice for understanding; If thou you sleekest her as silver, and searchest for her as for hid treasures; Then shalt thou understand the fear of the Lord, and find the knowledge of God. For the Lord giveth wisdom: out of his mouth cometh knowl-edge and understanding.

Intentional Misrepresentation

She told lies so they could feel as though she was better and in order for her to advance above the others and to achieve her goals. If she thought someone could outperform her, she would sabotage that person's final performance by saying mean things to get inside of their minds so that they felt less confident and insecure. When it was time for her to perform, their lack of confidence boast hers and gave her the strength and edge she needed to outperform them. She was a clever talker and could tell by the responses of her puppet friends that they were weak and depended on her. She also took the advantage of her friends by persuading them to believe not only in her, but also in her philosophy. She said the way she said it happened was the truth or that they should not listen to other people because the other people are idiots and not on her level. She intentionally misrepresented herself so that she could appeal as the one who knows it all and could not be outperformed.

Although she intentionally misrepresented herself, she knew there was nothing her friends could do to help when it was time to audition. One of her friends went out of his way to help her by telling the audition director all these great qualifications and experiences that she has in the industry. In the meanwhile, the director checked her profile and learned that she had a history of intentionally misrepresenting herself and fabricating her level of experiences. The director finished the process and allowed her to audition for an acting role. Once the audition was concluded, she later received a notice from the industry stating that her performance was overwhelmingly acceptable, but due to her intentional misrepresentation, she was declined the acting role.

She learned that life and death is in the power of the tongue and that what she had been doing, provoked an end to her promising career. She asked her friends for forgiveness for the way she treated them and for intentionally misrepresenting herself.

So, I am sending you this book in regards to *Life's Apologies.*

Discouraged Mindset

People must take control of their lives. When people do not have as much say or input in their lives as they would like, they become discouraged. If the mind is not emotionally fit, it can be kidnapped by outside negative influencers or invaders that are discouraging. When a person is disheartened, discouragement becomes a key factor that caused turmoil. People will become frustrated for whatever reasons, and if they do not have one, they will find one. People should be thankful they have a job and love the work they do, but lately they seemed to be getting everything right until an important deadline was missed.

There could be a number of things that caused the missed deadline to include being unhappy at home and at work. This possibly meant that the problem at home, poor work performance, and lack of effective communications was the source of the discouragement. Distractions from both home and work will cause fatigued, feeling of being overworked, and left with little or no self-esteem. The chance of people becoming emotionally discouraged to the point where they lack motivation and just want to be left alone, especially when the odds are against them and not in their favor, will increase. Those who are spiritually inclined met with their ministry and relied on the congregation for spiritual comfort to be released from fears of failure that may have caused their discouragement. When those who are experiencing discouragement also become emotionally and phys-ically drained, they become fatigued, and this prevents them from reaching their full potential.

If people would have faith and wish to turn their lives around, they must take on a willing and able attitude that could encourage them to be committed to achieving their goals. If they continue to lack confidence and display anger and hopelessness, it will be impossible for others to deal with them, and they will have further prob-lems that will have interfere with them reaching their full potential and achieving their goals.

There are things that can be done to assist those with transitioning to a better place in life if they are willing. Receiving plenty of rest shall allow the mind to rejuvenate so it can be refreshed. Mind free of clouded and negative discouragements have contributed to a better life. After rejuvenation, issues may be easier to be dealt with. People sometimes do not understand why it is so difficult for them to meet goals that they set out to achieve, and therefore they become blinded by an unknown cause that is affecting them. In spite of the odds, a developed cheerful attitude will ultimately lead people to become enthusiastic. Their lives will be more organized, and discouragement will become a thing of the past.So, I am sending you this book in regards to *Life's Apologies*.

God Help Me

God help me please because I do not know what I have done to my family. One night me my wife and our two kids woke up to a burning house and both of our cars had been damage to no repair. We called my brother, and just as I thought, I was reminded of being told about the people that I had been associated with. My brother went on to say that real friends speak the truth, but during the process, a friend or family member may be lost because of failing to listen. My brother also went on to say that my friend and family will become my enemies and I would have caused it.

Unfortunately, we had to live with my brother, which was better than being outdoors. My wife had no idea why this happened, but my brother and I did. I thought I was in love with another man's wife, and my wife was the only one who did not know. Although the husband had warned me, the other woman and I continued with our affair. Then one day, the man gunned me down on the streets in front of my wife and our sons and then said, "I warned you to stop having an affair with my wife." I heard those last words as I laid there on the streets, and the man walked away. When I woke up from comatose, I reached out for my wife's hand, but she refused to comfort me.

We continued to live with my brother, and I was reminded that I took what was sacred between us and allowed it to become tarnish. The only thing I could do was cry out to God and I said, "God help me please." I asked God to forgive me for what I had done and I repented of my sins. When I broke the covenant between my wife and me, I uprooted our family and destroyed it. I threw away the most treasured thing I had to live for, my wife and sons. I suddenly realized that what I had been searching for on the outside, I already had on the inside. Every single day, I ask my wife for forgiveness and I apologized to her each time.So, I am sending you this book in regards to *Life's Apologies*.

Being Incarcerated

Mom, Dad, and to the rest of the family, being incarcerated was not a part of the plan. People who have been incarcerated for some period can attest that it was indeed a traumatic experience. It must not be assumed that while in prison, inmates are in safe haven and only have to do chores and complete their convicted sentence. Adjusting to incarceration can be cruel, and some inmates had problems prior to their imprisonment. After being behind bars, they would encounter additional problems they did not anticipate. Some inmates, immediately upon being incarcerated, were met with the challenge of defending themselves in order to survive. They had to trade their personal hygiene items for protection to seal a sense of survival. They went without food to keep from being bullied and abused. Inmates also gave up money they earned or was given by family, just to retain their protection against being beaten and raped.

While being incarcerated, not only did inmates need protection to ward off physical abuse, they also needed counseling on how to cope with depression, knowledge of prison violence and experiences, and psychological disorders. If the inmates are forced to fight back and defend themselves but refused to submit to the demands of other inmates, this could cost them their lives. They must appear strong and ready to fight for their right to live life behind bars as an incarcerated inmate and not as an animal. Ultimately, if inmates refused to meet demands of other inmates and failed to protect themselves, it could be detrimental and may lead to a state of emotional pain, shock, and then helplessness.

Inmates while incarcerated, as a means for survival and protection, fought back because they hoped to be placed in solitary confinement once the incident was reported to the guards. When inmates fail to comply to meet the demands of other inmates, they took a chance on their survival, which should have been seriously considered. Incarcerated inmates must weigh their alternatives of possibly killing an inmate or being killed if they fought back. Either way, a life would be taken.

Being incarcerated means not only life behind bars, but also to learn what it would take in order to survive. This means that trades are made between inmates who are trying to defend themselves behind bars in order to survive. People should always do what it takes to avoid incarceration, and life behind bars will then be an afterthought.

I apologize to my mom and dad and the rest of my family for the embarrassment I caused them due to my incarceration.

So, I am sending you this book in regards to *Life's Apologies*

Stay Strong.

Strength means to keep going regardless of the opposition. Some people will prey on you and wish you would give up on yourself. The goal is to doubt and second guess yourself as a strong person with good character and attributes that will enable you to be whatever you want to be. When you are faced with opposition, you have to lean on God for intervention. The more you lean on Him, the easier it gets during the midst of your opposition. The oppositionist then becomes confused because you demonstrate that you have strength.

When you appear to be weak, people will take advantage of you. Once a new love is found or the money has dissipated, the person becomes disgruntled and manifests an argument to create an excuse to move on after you have been bled dry. It can be a friend, a relative, or a significant other, it does not matter. After this experience occurs, some people result to seeking counseling because of negative feelings such as low self-esteem appearing to be weak and being labeled. When people withdraw and the mind becomes locked in a box without a way out, the person then becomes suicidal. People also become mentally weak instead of mentally strong because of failing to identify with what is necessarily strong. Those who fail to have courage and show strength also become inferior and lose personal power and then fail to take positive risk or readily adapt to change.

The last thing a person should do is give up after multiple failures. Do not feel sorry for yourself! Get up and start all over again. If you would like to persevere through challenging circumstances, you must show your mental toughness. This is how you gather your strength. Your strength should derive from how well you control and manage your emotions and not allow someone else to do it for you. If you do not have the mental strength, it takes to follow your own rules and values, and then you become vulnerable to be controlled by someone else. If a person wants to rob a bank but not alone, the approach would be to get the friend that will not say no, and that will give up control. Your mental strength will also require you to be committed to yourself. You should have the willpower to say, "I can pass this test, I can win this race, or I am my own person and no one will take that away." You do not have to apologize to anyone for the strength that you develop; however, you should apologize if you abuse and take advantage of others.So, I am sending you this book in regards to *Life's Apologies*.

Chapter 12

Life's Apologies

Destiny's Path

Genesis 28:14

And thy seed shall be as the dust of the earth, and thou shalt spread abroad to the west, and to the east, and to the north, and to the south: and in thee and in thy seed shall all the families of the earth be blessed.

Acts 3:19

Repent ye therefore, and be converted, that your sins may be blotted out, when the times of refreshing shall come from the pres-ence of the Lord;

Numbers 14:17-18

And now, I beseech thee, let the power of my Lord be great, according as thou hast spoken, saying, The Lord is longsuffering, and of great mercy, forgiving iniquity and transgression, and by no means clearing the guilty, visiting the iniquity of the fathers upon the children unto the third and fourth generation

1 John 4:18

There is no fear in love; but perfect love casteth out fear: because fear hath torment. He that feareth is not made perfect in love.

Prosperous Achiever

As my sister and I grew up together, I noticed how different we were treated by our parents. I was treated the same when friends of the family visited us, but my sister was singled out as the flawless and prettiest one who had the looks that could be her ticket to success. All the while, during the conversations, I was overlooked as though I was invisible. I observed that my parents treated my older sister as a favorite and would at the same time undermine my existence and showed me no compassion. I concluded that my skin because my sister has a fair skin complexion and mine is less contributed to my parents not wanting to recognize me.

After my sister graduated from college and became a lawyer, my parents regarded me as contagious. Without hesitation, my parents would give in to the demands of my sister by doing unnecessary shopping for expensive items, knowing the family could not afford it.

Despite my sister and I having the same biological parents, it just so happened that I was born a little tan. I am proud of my tannest, but I do not think my parents are. What hurt me the most was when my parents failed to recognize my existence and my worth. I envied the fact that my sister became a prosperous achiever. My sister's feelings of being better than most are based on the way our parents raised her, and it is the fault of my parents that my sister has this overwhelming perception because of being a prosperous achiever who is above others.

Later, I concluded that my parents were the ones responsible for my sister being a horrible person despite being a prosperous achiever. Since my parents never embraced me as being beautiful and privileged, I developed a complex against my tannest, which almost resulted in me not becoming a well-respected, prosperous achiever.

I hope my sister will forgive me for being envious. For this reason, I apologize to my sister for envying the fact of being a prosperous achiever. To my sister, please accept my apologies for blaming you for what you were destined to be.So, I am sending you this book in regards to *Life's Apologies.*

Powerless Decision

My friend and I grew up and did almost everything together. Because I knew how to persuade my friend, I always made decisions for both of us. Although my friend wanted to go to a different college from me, it was my final decision that we went go to the same one. Once I made the final decision, I never once got the impression that my friend still disagreed with me about the college. However, our decision to attend the same college had fallen prey to my friend's inability to make a decision and stick with it. My friend's decision to attend a different college became powerless because I would always come up with the reason why we should side with the one I wanted.

When we got to college, we stayed in the same dorm room at my request. I always went to parties, so one Friday evening, I convinced my friend to go to a party with me. Once again, my decision overpowered the powerless decision and then we went to the party. While at the party, I persuaded my friend to have fun. We met another student at the party, whom I sexually assaulted. My friend was unaware of what I had done until after being identified and arrested as being the one who had committed the assault. If my friend was able to follow through with the decision not attend the party, this crime would be unfounded and the situation would not exist. Hopefully, this experience taught my friend not to be overtaken by powerless decisions.

When a decision is made and then changed because of being influenced, that person's decision is powerless. I have taken a stand and admitted to my friend that I committed the assault and it was wrong. I could not allow my friend to be penalized for the assault. I just wanted to apologize and I hope my apology will be accepted.So, I am sending you this book in regards to *Life's Apologies*.

Lenient Behavior

When receiving charity from any organization, some people allow pride to stand in the way of receiving the help they need. Most people who understand the meaning of charity are less likely to turn it down when they need assistance. The assistance does not necessarily have to come from a charity organization. There are many people who have a good heart and a giving spirit that enables them to willingly give without having any hesitations.

When people of their own free will help others in the community, they let them know that they care. People in the community come together and provide assistance. They also improve the envi-ronment and stabilize those who are experiencing less fortunate situations. Goods and charity are provided to family, friends, and some-times to people they do not know. On some occasions, good-spirited people make charitable gestures by paying for the food of some who do not have enough money.

There are some churches that will pay rent or utilities for those who are a part of their organization and are unable to. Other organizations that are linked to serving others such as Goodwill and the Salvation Army both are thrift shops that receive donations such as clothes and appliances in turn sell gently worn clothes at a reduced and affordable price to those who are in need.

There are nonprofit organizations that reach out to needy peo-ple in the community in order to serve them. Most nonprofit organizations provide giveaways and conduct events within the community without making a profit, but they do conduct fundraisers and solicit sponsorship to maintain stability. These organizations also reach out to the community to support veterans with their special needs. Within the community, the amount of charity received can also be based on the amount of income that a household may receive on a monthly basis.

People are barely surviving on their minimum income, and without assistance from charitable and nonprofit organizations, they would not survive. When people lack the resources and assistance needed, they are more likely to do whatever it takes to get what they need in order to feed their families.

Charity organization can be good and effective for the purpose of supporting communities in order to reach families and people who are in need of assistance. It is always good to know that people who are in need of assistance are able to reach out to charity organizations. These organizations and good-spirited people keep people within the communities reaching out and pulling together to assist each other. So, I am sending you this book in regards to *Life's Apologies*.

Betrayal and Gossip

People failed to realize that moral character was driven by their integ-rity. Those that are of poor character do not have good integrity. Having integrity meant that people of honor valued their moral character and understood that it would not be negotiated. There are certain people on the job that create nothing but gossip and drama, and every time there is an issue, that person's name is always at the center of the distraction. Even among family or friends, some people may have said, "Please do not mention this because it would be terrible consequences if it got out."

To entrust something very personal with a parent, a friend, a coworker, or even a counselor and then later learn that those very people cannot be trusted can be devastating. People like that have been dishonest. They have no integrity and refused to be blamed for betraying their friend. Whether in a sensitive job that required the highest level of integrity or a family go-to person, people have claimed to be trustworthy and still at the same time they pretended to exercise sound integrity with moral character. Not knowing what is meant by having integrity could definitely bring an end to seemingly perfect relationships. The negative impact of not knowing has disrupted family and best-friends relationships in the past.

Best friends are supposed to be able to trust each other. In this particular case, a friend was betrayed by her best friend whom she confined in. The best friend gossip to coworkers that the friend had told her that she was having an affair and was pregnant from someone other than her husband. At first, the best friend, whom was told of the affair, adamantly denied ever breaking the trust. In the meanwhile, the friend was placed in a moral dilemma, because she had no idea that her best friend could not be trusted. The best friend finally admitted that she betrayed her friend when she broke their bond of trust. Now she is apologizing to her friend because she was dishonest and betrayed her. So, I am sending you this book in regards to *Life's Apologies*.

Generational Failure

It is hard to be in the company of others who do not care if they are a failure. It seems like everyone enjoys their failing circumstances and always criticizes others for not wanting to be a failure or for wanting to make something of their lives. Most of the families in the area are mediocre and do not want to do better. Parents struggle to make ends meet, and the children are constantly in and out of trouble. Other relatives are also doing the very minimum to get by, and everyone is looking for a hustle. They do not care if they graduate from high school or college, or even make their next family generation better than the one before. Instead, they give up hope and do not think beyond the basics of paying bills, utility, sleeping, and eating.

To be a failure is a personal choice, and there are some who will make others feel as though they are already failures. Most of these people are satisfied with having a failure mentality. If people would stay positive, they will survive emotional thoughts of becoming a failure, and therefore have the courage to beat the odds of being a failure.

Courage will give them the fortitude to close doors on those who contribute to failure and open doors to those who will provide positive influences that will not allow failure. What it means is that failures are nothing more than challenges and tests that will lead to positive beginnings. Remember, submitting to failure is optional but not a way of life. Failing can also be a result of excuses that people make in order to continue to allow them to keep failing. However, people can only do so much to prevent failure when there are barely enough resources to make a difference.

To my one and only family, please forgive and accept this overdue apology for totally blaming them for not being able overcome most of their failures.So, I am sending you this book in regards to *Life's Apologies*.

Restoring Discipline

You may have one of the most undisciplined adolescent children that can be imagined, but do not worry, because you are not alone. No matter what you said, or how hard you tried to lead your adolescent child down the correct path, there seemed to be another person inside of their brains that continued to lash out. The more you gave, the less obedient, the less caring, and the more selfish your adolescence became. You provided basic needs of food, shelter, and cloth-ing, and you took it a step further by providing transportation and other nice to have items. You thought you were being too hard and therefore continued to reward the misbehavior. As a result, your adolescent child became more disrespectful and used profane language. Whether you abided by your adolescent's invisible rules, you began to second-guess yourself by trying to make sense of what mistakes you may have made. You ruminated over if you should have pressed harder to enforce your standards before things got out of hand. Also, because of your anguish, you mulled over who was being disciplined. Was it you, the parent, or was it your adolescent child?Sometimes when the situation of having an adolescent child who cannot be disciplined has gotten out of control, it is time for some form of inter-vention. A family discussion of concerned issues may be reasonable, or the thought of a professional family counselor would have been great and should have happened well before now. To turn your adolescent child over to someone else to deal with in hopes that some sense would be made of a bad situation may not be the ideal thing to do. It could actually cause more problems than less, and you could be perceived by the adolescent and others as being a failure. Having weighed your options to seek professional family counseling on how to cope with an adolescent child with behavioral problems will inad-vertently enable you and your adolescent child the ability to experience restored discipline within the family. The problem that you were currently facing with did not happen overnight, and there was absolutely no need for you to apologize for trying to do what is right. Through all the chaos on both sides, there was plenty of room for apologies. Your adolescent child cannot be disciplined without help, and Dr. Phil voiced his opinionated view on possible cause and effect on parents and the adolescent who is undisciplined.

The most logical stride to take if your adolescent child has misbehaved out of character is to invest in professional family counseling before the situation becomes a catastrophe. It could be detrimental to wait before counseling is received because of the possible underling cause that contributed to the lack of discipline by the adolescent child. It is better to have found the root of the problem, than use punishment as the initial option. An outlined plan that influence and enable the adolescent child to consequently get back on the correct path of being well-disciplined will enhance the achievement of positive goals. In the interim, by apologizing and showing understanding and love, the adolescent child and the parent can both reach a middle ground and learn to accept and respect each other's position.So, I am sending you this book in regards to *Life's Apologies*.

Give Wisdom

Regardless of the circumstances, your child is human and has feelings the same as you or anyone else. Do not reject or throw your child away just because of not being a model child. In fact, this child is the one that needs the most from you. A lot of times, people fail to see the good in children because of focusing too much on the negative. Do not always focus on the negative things that your child is doing. Your child is the one that needs the most attention and guidance rom you. Life is not perfect, but underneath the dust, you were dealt a blessed hand.

Everyone is created uniquely in God's image, but God does not expect your child to be perfect, and neither should you. Instead of overwhelming your child with expectations, just remember that your child may not be as emotionally strong as you may feel. If you neglect to provide nurturing to that child, you could cause further emotional trauma; therefore, you should immediately seek counseling. Counseling can determine as to the underlining cause for your child going off course. You owe it to your child to embrace and show empathy, and to be understanding as to why there is frustration.

In the meanwhile, reach out and continue to embrace your child by letting the child know that you do care. Your other children may be doing well, but know that you will be put under the microscope, and how you respond to the situation of the one that needs the most attention will also dictate the chances of mending relationships within the family. Do not look down on or be judgmental! Just be there because this child needs you most and more than the others. Although the situation could be worst, you should apologize to your child for allowing it to get to this point. Trust me. You will never forgive yourself if you do not apologize.So, I am sending you this book in regards to *Life's Apologies.*

My Abortion

In this book, *Life's Apologies*, I bookmarked the page that read 'My Abortion' and sent the book to my mother because I want to tell her the truth about my abortion which she knew nothing about. I began like this, Mom on Resurrection morning when you came to wake me up; I was not there because the day before, I went to the next county over to have an abortion. I regretted my situation and was ashamed. I was also disappointed and it bothered me that I did not come to you for support. Nevertheless, I still want you to know that during the time of the abortion, I did not runaway, I had complications and had to be hospitalized and that is why I was not home. Since I had complications during the abortion, I thought I would not be able to get pregnant again, but that is not the case and I am doing well. I can only thank God that my wrongdoing turned out for my good, because I learned a lesson and it could have been worst. I also thank God that I am still able to have children. When I became pregnant I turned to my boyfriend, who was not supportive, so I made the choice to have an abortion which I knew was the best decision for me at the time. Only at the right time and under better circumstances such as marriage, I will become pregnant again. Therefore, mom please forgive me and I apologize for not trusting in you.

So, I am sending you this book in regards to *Life's Apologies.*

ABOUT THE AUTHOR

Carolann Murray was born and raised in DeLand, Florida. After she graduated from High School, she enlisted in the all-volunteer Unit-ed States Army and retired with honorable service. Before leaving Florida to serve her country, Murray made a personal commitment to serve God through her faith and belief that He would never leave her nor forsake her. When not consumed by her nonprofit orga-nization *Life's Apologies*, Inc., Murray continue to work on other writing projects, and she loves spending quality time with family, and especially her grandchildren. The web address for *Life's Apologies* is lifesapologiesorg@ gmail.com